Ritual
and
Pastoral Care

THEOLOGY AND PASTORAL CARE SERIES

edited by
Don S. Browning

ELAINE RAMSHAW

Ritual and Pastoral Care

Don S. Browning, *editor*

THEOLOGY AND PASTORAL CARE

FORTRESS PRESS
PHILADELPHIA

Library of Congress Cataloging-in-Publication Data

Ramshaw, Elaine, 1956–
  Ritual and pastoral care.

  (Theology and pastoral care series)
  Bibliography: p.
  1. Pastoral theology. 2. Liturgics.   I. Browning, Don
S. II. Title. III. Series.
  BV4011.R36 1987   253   85-45487
  ISBN 0-8006-1738-X

2098G86   Printed in the United States of America   1-1738

for Thomas Droege
whose caring has the constancy of ritual
whose ritual has the tenderness of care

Contents

Acknowledgments

I would like to thank the following people for the stories of rituals that became illustrations in this book: Michelle Bakalyar, Philip Blackwell, Marie Coglianese, Kristine DeYoung, Thomas Droege, Burton Everist, Norma Everist, Carolyn Groves and her daughter Monica, Larry Hofer, Clark Hyde, Barbara Lundblad, John Nelson, Kendra Nolde, John Northcott, Gail Ramshaw-Schmidt and her daughters, Miriam and Monica, Cecilia Reed, Julie Ryan, Scott Stoner, and David Truemper.

Series Foreword

Our purpose in the Theology and Pastoral Care Series is to present ministers and church leaders with a series of readable books that will (1) retrieve the theological and ethical foundations of the Judeo-Christian tradition for pastoral care, (2) develop lines of communication between pastoral theology and the other disciplines of theology, (3) create an ecumenical dialogue on pastoral care, and (4) do this in such a way as to affirm yet go beyond the recent preoccupation of pastoral care with secular psychotherapy and the other social sciences.

The books in this series are written by authors who are well acquainted with psychology, psychotherapy, and the other social sciences. All of the authors affirm the importance of these disciplines for modern societies and for ministry in particular, but they see them also as potentially destructive of human values unless they are guided in their practical application by tested religious and ethical traditions. But to retrieve the best of the Judeo-Christian tradition for the church's care and counseling is a challenging intellectual task—a task to which few writers in the area of pastoral care have attended with sufficient thoroughness. This series addresses that task out of a broad ecumenical stance, with all of the authors taking an ecumenical approach to theology. Besides a vigorous investigation of Protestant resources, there are specific treatments of pastoral care in Judaism and Catholicism.

We hope that the series will help ministers and church leaders view afresh the theological and ethical foundations of care and counseling. All of the books have a practical dimension, but even more important than that, they help us see care and counseling differently. Compared with writings of the last thirty years in this field, some of the books will seem startlingly different. They will need to be read and pondered with care. But I have little doubt that the series will make a profound and lasting impact upon the way we understand and practice our care for one another.

Elaine Ramshaw teaches on the faculty of the Methodist Theological School of Ohio. I believe that all who read her prose and savor the ease and polish with which she sets forth her ideas will readily agree that we have much to look forward to in the theological writings which will gradually come forth from her pen. Although near the beginning of her career in theological teaching and writing, Elaine Ramshaw writes about ritual and pastoral care with the authority of one with decades of experience and reflection.

In *Ritual and Pastoral Care* we have a book that stands nearly alone in the effort to unearth the pastoral care dimensions of the liturgical life of the church. Years ago, Seward Hiltner tried to define pastoral care and pastoral theology as the shepherding or caring perspective brought to bear on all the minister's acts. This was his way of saying that everything the minister does—preaching, administration, education, worship and liturgy—all have caring or shepherding potential. Professor Ramshaw affirms this point of view and has advanced our thinking considerably about the care and shepherding potential of the ritual aspects of the Christian ministry.

There is much in this book to be reflected on and valued. There is solid theory about the relevance to care of various forms of ritual. There are discussions of the care dimensions of corporate ritual. There are novel presentations of the caring aspects of individual or personal ritual acts between minister and lay persons or directly between the laity. But the great artistry of this book is in the wide range of beautifully presented illustrations of how ritual does, or could, convey care for the individual, the community, and the world. This book simultaneously has a simplicity and a profundity that will give it enduring value for years to come.

DON S. BROWNING

Sacred Ritual
and
Human Need

A pastor I know was installed some years ago at a church where the eucharist is celebrated weekly. After a while my friend, still only beginning to sort out all the new faces, thought he noticed a woman who came faithfully every week but never seemed to come up for Communion. One day, though, a few months after his installation, he saw her for the first time at the table. When he talked with her afterward, she confirmed that this had been the first time she'd gone to communion since he came, and added that in fact she had not communed for many years. Long ago she had gone through a bitter divorce, and she had felt since that her inability to forgive her husband or to overcome her anger at him was an obstacle which prevented her from coming to the Lord's Table. "But," she went on to explain, "the way you celebrate is so hospitable, it made it difficult for me not to come." Through every tone and gesture, my friend made it irresistibly clear that the whole service led to that tablesharing where the community was united, so that finally she just couldn't stay away.

I tell this story because I think it is an excellent illustration of the way pastoral care can be accomplished in and through ritual action. Discussions of pastoral care in recent decades have generally given ritual short shrift, and if they mention ritual at all, the focus tends to be the one-to-one rites such as confession or the laying on of hands. The "public" liturgical role of the pastor has often been dissociated from the "private," individualized, counseling role that is considered the essence of pastoral care. It is my conviction that the paradigmatic act of pastoral care is the act of presiding at the worship of the gathered community, and that this priority in no way contravenes the importance of the one-on-one, "private," counseling-oriented dimension of pastoral care or the psychological insights that today inform that dimension. Rather, the pastoral act of liturgical leadership supports this as well as other dimensions of pastoral caring, giving them the focus and experiential quality that clearly defines them as "pastoral." In this book I intend to explore the many ways and means of ritual care, as the pastor practices such care for the local community, for the individuals within that community, and for the world that community serves.

HEALING THE DIVISION BETWEEN "RITUALISTS" AND "COUNSELORS"

In a fine article on "The Use of Ritual in Pastoral Care," H. P. V. Renner gives a succinct summary of the mutual accusations which have divided the pastoral counselors from those he calls the "specialist ritualists." The counselor, says Renner, "too often feels that ritual lacks warmth and empathy; that its fixed forms are insensitive to 'where the patient is'; that it stanches free flow of a patient's feelings; that it 'generalizes' his or her experience; and that it tends to reduce pastoral ministry to the magical." In return, the ritualists have attacked counseling as an anaesthetic or palliative which attempts to treat symptoms in isolation from the total situation, sidestepping confrontation with the deeper issues raised by personal crisis. The counselor isolates the individual from community support and cuts her or him adrift from the stabilizing anchor of ritual.[1]

We all know too well the truths that give rise to these counteraccusations. Ritual can indeed be formalist, distancing, insensitive to the specificity or pace of the individual's needs, intent on enforcing a procrustean pattern. Equally sadly, even "pastoral" counseling can be privatized, narrowly focused on the needs of the moment, insufficiently grounded in the depths of the tradition, tone-deaf to mystery.

This book, however, is based on the belief that both formalist ritual and privatized counseling are distortions, and that if the proponents of ritual and counseling will stop attacking each other's characteristic distortions they will have much to contribute to each other's enrichment. Pastoral counseling can be imbued with a sense of community and of the transcendent; there is no surer way for this to happen than through a vital and self-conscious connection with the worship life of the community. Ritual can resonate to human need, and to this end there is much the ritualist can learn from the psychological insights into human development and personality familiar to those in the field of pastoral care.

This is not to say that psychological theory should become the new norm of the church's ritual practice. The pastoral counseling field has demonstrated the danger of letting psychology usurp theology's normative role in pastoral care. In much of the pastoral counseling literature, psychology is implicitly allowed to define both the problem and the solution, the nature of the predicament and the goal of human fulfillment. This co-opting of theology's role by psychological theory is a major factor underlying the distortions of pastoral counseling just discussed: the privatization, the focus on symptoms, the disregard for the transcendent. A recent move within the field has tried to correct this bias by a return to the rich symbolic resources of the theological tradition. The field of pastoral liturgy is taking direction from this example, making use of social scientific insights. It can even, in some sense, be transformed by these insights, without losing its theological integrity.

THE ROLE OF PSYCHOLOGY IN
PASTORAL RITUAL STUDIES

The self-understanding of Christian worship and sacramental practice must remain at heart a theological one. The norms of our ritual are grounded not in human need but in God. What we do (pray, proclaim, commune), with whom we do it (the community of the baptized), when (the Lord's day), and why (to show forth Christ's death and proclaim the resurrection) are all questions which are answered at ground level by theology in reflection on the Word of God. We do not extrapolate our Sunday worship or the sacraments from our "felt needs" or from any psychological theory. Rather, we are drawn and commanded to worship by the explicit instructions and the implicit world view we receive from the tradition. Our vision of the future reign of God, our ideal of Christian community and social justice, and our image of personal fulfillment through "sanctification" are all aspects of the theological world view which alone can adequately norm our worship.

We may find psychological theories whose implicit world views accord well in some respects with our theological vision, but they cannot replace it. Even on psychology's own ground, in matters of personal health and development, psychology must reach beyond itself into philosophical and metaphorical language to ground its image of human fulfillment. For the images that shape Christian ritual, that language must be theological, biblical, catholic, and confessional.

The norm of our ritual, then, is not our need but God's invitation. Yet it is also true that, as Victor White put it, "God's command to us to worship him is a concession to our needs."[2] We have remembered this better, perhaps, with regard to the sacraments than with regard to all regular community worship. We have focused on God's self-giving in the sacraments, but have too often talked as if regular worship were primarily our gift to God ("He gave you seven days; the least you can do is give him back one hour"). The emphasis on the "objective" character of worship as "duty" has made us lose sight of the equally theological and not at all "subjective" truth that the liturgy is God's gift to us: an activity God ordains out of a knowledge of our needs that runs deeper even than our own self-knowledge.

We can say, then, without giving ourselves over to psychological subjectivism, that sacred ritual serves human needs. On the level of exploring what those needs are and how ritual can answer them, both theological and psychological understandings can come into play. There are some human needs we deduce primarily from our theological understanding of human nature, such as the need for forgiveness. There is also, however, a broad range of human needs which we can understand better or even identify for the first time on the basis of the psychological study of human development and interaction. It is here that I see the main role of psychology in relation to pastoral care, whether that be expressed in counseling or in ritual. Pastoral care is care for human need, and psychology can tell us a great deal about human need from a different perspective: the study of pathology, of development, and of human "systems." As sociology can give us a different perspective on the visible church which may help us determine the causes and effects of various ecclesial polities, so psychology can enlarge our understanding of the ways our rituals do or do not meet our personal and communal needs.

One final thing must be said about this methodological question of the relation between theological and psychological points of view. I think it is necessary that each be allowed to critique the other in a serious way. It is easy to see how theology might critique a psychological view of human nature in light of a deeper awareness of mystery or a more radical sense of human sinfulness. Our perception and even our scientific investigation of our own needs may indeed be distorted at times by narcissism or sinful self-interest. It is equally likely, however, that our theological formulations may be pervasively distorted by self-interest, whether institutional or personal. Psychology may see the human consequences of some practice we have enshrined and call it into question on the basis that it does people harm. To listen to this challenge is not to hand over the normative function to psychology, for our own tradition supplies the impetus for theologians' self-critical awareness in its recognition that theologians, too, are finite and fallible. To take such a challenge seriously is, rather, to acknowledge that even when we think we are merely explicating revelation we may be constructing a rationale to legitimate our own self-interest, and that at times only a perspective from outside may be able to force us into recognizing the self-serving distortion of our thought.

THE CASE OF RITUAL LEADERSHIP: HIERARCHY OR MUTUALITY?

The issue of the nature of ritual leadership in the church is one which points up the polarities which can develop between the traditionally minded "ritualist" and the psychologically minded "counselor." The formalist stereotype has it that ritualists are highly invested in hierarchical authority, probably in order to enhance their own power by denigrating the layperson's unmediated experience of the divine. Ritualists are often suspected of wanting to corner the market on grace, to transmit the goods from God to parishioner through a graded sequence of authorities appointed from above.

In contrast to this stereotype of hierarchical ritual authority, contemporary theorists of pastoral care like to see the pastor's role as that of companion or co-traveler, who walks beside rather than stands above, who shuns artificial hierarchy in the cause of genuine mutuality. This image of the pastoral role is in part based on a sociopolitical ideology of democracy and egalitarianism, and in part reflects the "just-folks" coziness of the mass-media culture, where social distance is collapsed into instant first-name-basis familiarity. Even more immediately, though, the ideal of pastor as companion derives from the psychotherapeutic model, particularly the Rogerian model most influential on the pastoral counseling field. In Rogerian therapy the therapist eschews the old authoritative role of "Herr

Doktor" who doles out answers to cure the passive patient, and sets about learning rather how to listen with respectful and empathic attention. It was called "client-centered therapy," until even that term, by perpetuating the client-professional model, was felt to be too lacking in mutuality and "person-centered therapy" took its place. People trained in the tradition of pastoral care which has grown out of this influence can understandably have a hard time fitting ritual leadership into the pastor's role as listening companion or fellow traveler.

This perceived incompatibility of roles is, of course, in one aspect a contemporary recapitulation of the time-honored polarities of high church vs. low church, transcendence vs. immanence, vertical vs. horizontal, church as hierarchy vs. church as community. Like all these polarities, the one of hierarchy vs. mutuality in ritual leadership only becomes an irresoluble contradiction when the contrast is polemically overdrawn. It is a distortion to identify care for ritual with a stereotypical "high-church" defense of magical power over the laity, just as it is inaccurate to stereotype pastoral counseling types as exclusively concerned with their own states of mind and with making each other comfortable. Certainly there are those extreme ritualists who think that humanity was made for the Sabbath as also there are the extremes at the other end, who believe that the Sabbath was made for humanity in a bygone era, to pave the way for group therapy. But polemics aside, there is no inherent contradiction between the two images of the pastoral role. My own experience in worship at church-related colleges suggests that the professors who do the best leading the liturgy and preaching are usually the ones who do the most counseling: better listeners are potentially better presiders, for they know the needs of their people well.

Yet many pastors who have been trained to listen and to see themselves as co-travelers still have difficulty integrating ritual leadership into their view of the pastoral role. Paul Pruyser in an essay on benediction asks why many pastors nowadays cannot seem to bless with authority, and suggests that it is due to a weakening of belief in divine providence.[3] I would suggest that in many cases the difficulty lies in the polarization of hierarchical and mutual roles. Many people identify ritual leadership so closely with the extreme hierarchical end of the spectrum that they see the exercise of any sort of ritual power as destructive of mutuality. They are uncomfortable with defining the pastoral role in terms of ritual leadership because they understand ritual leadership as a vaguely medieval stance, smacking of magic and feudalism, filling some undefined needs perhaps, but not in an ideally person-centered way.

The unpolarized truth of the matter is that there are many styles of ritual power, some at the extreme of hierarchicalism and some with a profound sense of mutuality. I know a rabbi who bought in Israel a six-foot prayer shawl, which he wraps around people when he blesses them; he explained to me his preference for this act over a standard blessing by saying, "I don't have magic words or magic hands." He was rejecting, of course, a manner of blessing which he identified with the hierarchical pole of power-from-above, where the clergy stands on high and passes down parcels of grace. If my friend were to think, however, that in wrapping the tallith around someone in blessing he is not performing an act of great ritual power—not exercising ritual authority—then he would be naïve. His action is, in fact, a striking image of how ritual authority can be exercised in and with a vivid sense of fellow-humanity. It is his tallith, it is from Israel, and he brings the other into this symbol of their common prayer, their shared tradition, their communal hope. It is a good image of what the Christian pastor tries to do for those in need—to invite them into, to surround them with, to wrap them in the symbols of our common salvation.

NORMS FOR THE EXERCISE
OF RITUAL POWER

Judaism and Christianity share a critical appreciation for the potential misuse of the vehicles of human religious experience. The exercise of ritual power is certainly one of those expressions of human religiosity which is ambiguous in relation to the aims of Israel's God. Like all other ambiguous religious acts, the exercise of ritual power must be judged by norms which alone can authenticate or unmask it; justice, kindness, humility are the norms suggested by the prophet Micah. In a Christian critique of human religiosity, Gordon Lathrop says that the symbols and acts of human religious aspirations can be used in Christian worship, but only if they are "broken at the foot of the cross." The symbols of religious hope are "broken," he says, because they are fulfilled in that least religious and least hopeful of all events—the crucifixion.⁴ The symbolic act of ritual leadership, as when a pastor lays hands on a person who kneels before her, is "broken" when the meaning of leadership is understood to be fulfilled in the cross. What is the symbol of Christ's leadership? The symbol of a leader whose life was given in service, a leader whose followers had deserted and whose cause was lost. Hardly a happy case for hierarchical security!

Yet neither the self-critical strand in our tradition nor the judgment of the cross has prevented Christian pastors from blithely exercising power at others' expense. Here, as I indicated earlier, lies the necessity of considering a critique from without. As sociology can expose oppressive uses of power by ecclesial structures, so psychology can identify unhealthy forms of authority in the church. In most cases where one individual exercises ritual leadership, for instance, there is some echo in the authority role of a parent-child relationship. According to Erik Erikson, this ritual echo of an infantile relationship can be used in a healthy or unhealthy way. Either it can evoke and reaffirm the participants' basic sense of trust and providence in a way that will undergird mature responsibility, or it can infantilize the participants and keep them dependent on the parent-figure for security and initiative. A particular practice of ritual leadership in the church could coexist with the rhetoric of Christian freedom and maturity, and yet actually encourage emotional dependency; if a psychological study could prove this, it would be grounds for calling the practice into question.

The norms for Christian ritual, including the character of ritual authority, are finally, however, judged not on psychological but on philosophical and theological grounds. They will vary somewhat according to different theological traditions within the church, so that there is no way in a non-confessional book such as this one to make constructive statements about those norms which will apply for all readers. Yet there are certain broad, biblically based themes which may be applicable across the spectrum. Authority in the church is based on sheer grace, on the promise of the Word, not on any personal qualities of the clergy—that was decided in the Donatist controversy. (My own Lutheran way of making this point would be to say, the only evangelical authority is that which makes the promise trustable.) Authority is defined in relation to the community, for whether a church body's polity is more hierarchical or more congregational, the liturgy has always been theologically understood as the work of the whole people of God, and the main sacraments as every Christian's baptismal birthright. Leadership is defined by service, even if most of us no longer practice footwashing as a sacrament as Ambrose did. And the paradigm for presiding at the eucharist is that of gracious invitation: come and enter into the realm of God, where the royal banquet, the wedding feast, is spread for tax-collectors and sinners and the poor dragged in off the street.

This image of eucharistic hospitality draws us back to the story with which I began this chapter, the story of my friend and his divorced parishioner. My friend exercised a very persuasive form of ritual power. A good presider, he acted not as a vicarious substitute to do the people's work for them, nor as a drill sergeant to enforce compliance, but as a focal figure to draw people into his actions and through that action point them to God. He met the woman's particular need without knowing beforehand what it was, and that opened the way for a conversation where he could offer also a counselor's care. In conversation and in ritual he was doing the same thing: conveying the invitation of God through and to their shared humanity, and drawing her into the symbols of salvation.

CHAPTER 1

Ritual and Care
for
the Community

LITURGY AND HUMAN NEED

While the paradigmatic act of pastoral care is presiding at the worship of the assembly, it is important to remember that *liturgy* etymologically means the work of the people, not the work of the pastor. The pastor's work is to midwife the labor of the people of God. She presides, leads, directs, and organizes, all to help the people of God do *their* work. She coaches them in the various skills necessary to their work: the lectors' reading, the assistant ministers' speaking or chanting, the whole assembly's movement and singing and phrasing of petitions in prayer. A good presider is not one who force-feeds rubrics to people, like small helpings of a dried-out tradition; a good presider is one who draws her congregation into the ancient dance with a new song. When such a pastor leaves her congregation, the people look for a pastor who will enter with them into the liturgical tradition they have come to appropriate as their own. Throughout all the following discussion of ritual care for the community, then, it should be remembered that the pastor's responsibility is not to create a living liturgy single-handedly. Rather, the pastor's role is to assist in the people's creative task, through her knowledge of the church's liturgical tradition and the people's ritual needs.

In the first section of this chapter, I will discuss several of the fundamental human needs which can be met in part by a healthy ritual practice. I will consider ritual as a way to establish order, to reaffirm meaning, to bond community, to handle ambivalence, and to encounter mystery. The purpose of this discussion, as was made clear in the introduction, is not to focus the church's liturgy on the pursuit of any and all human wishes. The normative aim of the liturgy is not human comfort but the glory of God.

Yet "the dwelling of God is with humankind," which means that God has chosen to link divine glory and human need. The incarnational heart of our theology is what opens the way to a consideration of the human side of religious experience from secular human perspectives.

Knowledge of a psychological or anthropological perspective on ritual need will help a pastor understand his parishioners' reactions to change in the liturgy and other often apparently irrational feelings they have about worship. Even more fundamentally, such knowledge will give him a whole new set of questions to ask of his church's ritual practice. He will certainly ask the theological questions: Does it show forth the grace of the Gospel? Does it attend to the whole of the paschal mystery, cross as well as resurrection? Does it reflect the justice of the Reign of God? But in dialogue with these questions will be another set of questions, asking how the ritual responds to the generic human needs that surface in ritual situations. The different perspectives can keep each other honest by mutual questioning. If a congregation so settles into the comfortable enjoyment of its own warm community that it is deaf to the world outside, the theological concern for justice can question that self-satisfaction. On the other hand, if theological justifications allow the ritual practice of keeping children from the eucharist while calling them members of the community, a psychological look at the children's sense of exclusion can question the assumption that community is experienced as it is defined. Out of such mutual critique will come a ritual practice which is richer, more honest, and more faithful to its message.

THE NEED TO ESTABLISH ORDER

A ritual proper is a relatively formalized, corporate, symbolic act of ritualization. Ritualization is a much wider phenomenon, including all the aspects of our biosocial behavior that are patterned, repetitive, conventionalized. Without ritualization we would have to plan every action from scratch and analyze the meaning of every interaction, like the stereotyped psychoanalyst who responds to "Hello" by saying, "What do you mean by that?" Conventions and habits set us free to think about other things by putting many functions on a socially agreed-upon automatic pilot. They also reassure us by creating a sameness and familiarity in our experience, by reaffirming our place in the social order with conventions of recognition, and by letting us trust that the person stretching her hand out is not about to hit us.

All ritualization, then, is about the ordering of experience. This is a fundamental human need for emotional as well as pragmatic reasons. Anyone who doubts this has only to observe a toddler for a week. For all that little children show great spontaneity and creativity, it remains true that they have an insatiable desire for ritualization. The story must be read with the same words, the same inflection, and the same ritualized question-and-answer exchanges. The passion with which children insist on sameness shows their need for order, stability, and the reassurance of continuity in human interaction. What can I count on? What will be here tomorrow?

Ritualization can fail in two ways. If it breaks down, continuity is not maintained, expectations are frustrated, and the insecurity of chaotic, unpredictable experience takes over. On the other hand, if it is built up too rigidly, the healthy ordering of experience is threatened by overkill. Obsessive-compulsive ritualizations, such as continual handwashing, are the ultimate over-ritualizations, where the rigidity is absolute and prevents all freedom of activity. There is a wide range in healthy people's needs to order experience, from those who value greater spontaneity to those who appreciate more constancy. What is happening when the child asks for the seventeenth reading of the same story in a row is a clash between two different developmental levels of ritualization-need. The child lives with tremendous vulnerability and ambivalence she cannot yet integrate, and needs far more the reassurance of repeated, dependable interaction. Luckily, the healthy parent finds his child unaccountably fascinating, and this can usually offset the boredom of the requested routine.

No matter where an individual falls on the spectrum of need for continuity/spontaneity, healthy ritualization for that individual is always a balance between the poles, a flexible order. Even the ritualistic toddler shows this balance in, say, her enjoyment of Mr. Rogers' opening song. It is the small variations in the ritual that delight her in the context of the overall reassuring familiarity of word and music and action. Healthy ritualization is always like that, providing the stability of a dependable context within which variance can delight.

Formal corporate ritual is by definition more ordered than everyday ritualizations. There are several ways to answer "How are you?" but only one way to answer "The Lord be with you." People who value spontaneity and freedom of interaction very highly are naturally apt to experience all formal ritual as rigid and restrictive. What is true of all ritualization, however, remains true also of formal rituals: healthy rituals order experience flexibly. The greater formalization is necessary due to the corporate nature of the event, the symbolic weight it must bear, and the tradition it must pass on—but the principle of balance remains the same. Rigidity is a sign of sickness, of the perversion of ritual purpose. Psychologically, one would judge it a sign of specific defensiveness or generalized insecurity. It actually defeats the ordering purpose of ritual, because one cannot provide continuity through change by rigidly resisting all change.

The mistake of many pastors, however, is to read all resistance to liturgical innovation as rigidity, and to mock the conservative impulse. The need for order and continuity is fundamental to the ritual purpose. When people say "This is the way we have always done it," they are saying something very precious in our fast-changing, mobile society. Anyone who doesn't have deep respect for that hunger for continuity should not be messing around with other people's ritual practice. This does not mean, of course, that nothing can ever be changed. It does mean that, even more than in other areas of congregational life, the introduction of change in ritual practice must be gradual and respectful of the need for continuity of practice.

THE NEED TO REAFFIRM MEANING

As all ritualization orders experience, so all ritualization communicates some sort of meaning, even if that meaning is as simple a message as "I will act as is expected of me in this situation." Formal rituals carry the core meanings of the social group performing them, the meanings which determine that group's world view. They do this through the use of symbols which have many layers of significance and a wide range of interpretation. Through such symbols as a wooden cross or the act of giving bread or the community's forming a circle, we express the deepest meanings we know of, and often meanings deeper than we consciously know. The human need to make sense of experience is universal and fundamental. Faced with the biggest questions of life and death, love and evil, the origin and destiny of the human race and the universe, we cannot pin down an answer in logical formulas. We turn to symbolic expressions of our trust in that which grounds the goodness in our experience and shapes the tradition in which we make our meanings.

The need for the ritual expression and reinforcement of the symbolic world view is intensified in situations which threaten meaning or coherence. That is why people who go along without access to the tradition's symbols often turn to ritual in times of transition or tragedy. The taken-for-granted everyday world is disrupted, one's place in the social structure is shifted, a relationship one has depended upon for continuity is ended, or undeserved suffering strikes at one's assumptions about God's justice. Any of these changes threatens our world of meaning by showing the impermanence of all the continuities of day-to-day life that we usually rely on for support of our assumptions about who is important, what can be trusted, and how we should act. The positive way to state this intensified need for meaning is that such times make an opening in our lives for the large questions to break in and catch our attention. A major pastoral problem here is how to respond to people who seek out the church's ritual only at times of transition or tragedy. This problem will be touched on later in this chapter, in the section on sacraments as life-cycle rites.

It is ritual's role in affirming the central meaning–structure of the community which gives it normative, ethical force. Part of the symbolic world view presented in ritual is the tradition's understanding of good and evil, its models of the good person, its image of a just society. This normative dimension can never be separated out from the ritual functions of bonding the community or linking it with the transcendent. Even a ritual which has no explicit normative statement must carry implicit assumptions and images of what is right and valued. This means, for instance, that one cannot bless any activity without raising the normative question of how that activity—whether battle, inauguration, or second marriage—conforms to the tradition's understanding of justice and love. In these times when there is so much pluralism within the church on ethical issues, this normative dimension of ritual leads to great confusion over decisions of ritual practice. Some of these issues will be illustrated later in this chapter, particularly in the discussion on rituals of divorce.

There is an even broader, more fundamental pastoral concern raised by the connection between ritual and the human need for meaning. That is the concern for honesty in the church's ritual expression. The power of ritual to communicate meaning is vitiated when ritual is known to lie or to contradict clear experience. Of course, there are differences in interpretation, and some people may call a lie what others would call an expression of hope, but outright dishonesty should be avoided whenever possible.

There are three kinds of dishonesty which threaten ritual's credibility as a carrier of meaning. The first and most blatant type is for the ritual to make statements about the participants which are widely at variance with their real-life situations. A common example of this occurs in adolescent rites of confirmation or believer's baptism, when the rhetoric of free choice clashes with many teenagers' experience of strong familial or peer pressure to go through with the rite. At the same time the language of lifelong commitment and adult membership does not fit well with a thirteen-year-old's experience of his readiness to make permanent commitments, or of adult church members' willingness to accept him as an equal in decision-making. All this does not mean that there should be no rite of adolescence, but only that we should be honest about what we intend it to mean. Such marked discrepancies between ritual word and experienced reality only encourage the tendency of some young people to see ritual as a sign of the hypocrisy of the institutional church.

The second kind of dishonesty common in ritual is related to the first, though somewhat more subtle. It is the untruthfulness which is risked whenever the worship leader imputes certain feelings to the congregation, in an attempt to make the prayer more personal and relevant. While it can have that effect for those whose feelings are accurately described, it can also alienate the rest of the assembly. Liturgical scholars call this the mistake of subjectivization, and they object to it not only because it risks inaccuracy and alienation, but also for the more theological reason that it focuses prayer on the praying person's state of mind, rather than on prayer's proper object, the work of God. For both these reasons, it is better not to state in public prayer that we are happy to be here today, or that we feel burdened with guilt over our government's actions in Central America or over our own internecine quarrels. Even at such a rite as a funeral, it is better not to assume too much about the people's state of mind. One can ask God to deal graciously with those who mourn, for all those present are mourners by definition, but attempts to describe "our" feelings of sadness, confusion, or anger are unlikely to seem honestly fitting to everyone praying.

The third common cause of ritual dishonesty is the manipulation of forcing people on the spot into ritual statements which they are not inclined to make. One such situation was described recently in an anonymous letter to *The Lutheran*:

> . . . I inwardly recoil whenever I read or hear of a church service during which the pastor unexpectedly calls for all married couples to stand and publicly renew their wedding vows. If my former spouse and I had been placed in such an embarrassing position, we would have hated ourselves for our hypocrisy.

Undoubtedly pastors who initiate these little rituals do so with the best of intentions. For those couples who are already lovingly committed to each other, this can be a beautiful reinforcement to their marriage. But it is unreasonable to expect a healing of a dying relationship through such one-shot, show-biz techniques.[1]

This letter demonstrates the danger of springing ritual statements on people without their prior consent. Whenever one wishes to get people to participate in ritual statements beyond those implied in their coming to the service, one should check with them beforehand and involve them in planning the ritual. It may be assumed that the families' support for a marriage is implied in their attending the wedding, and therefore it is probably all right to ask them corporately to state that support (though it would always be best to talk over the meaning of that statement with all concerned in advance). On the other hand, one cannot assume the willingness of everyone present at the Sunday service to affirm the new lease on life Mary and John have achieved through divorce, no matter how true or worthy of affirmation this may be.

Children are especially vulnerable to others' control, and therefore one must be particularly careful to avoid manipulating them in ritual situations. In rites marking the divorce or second marriage of a child's parent(s), or the blessing or baptism of his new sibling, the child should as far as possible be given freedom to decide beforehand what he wants to do or say, and not be forced into saying nice things welcoming his new stepfather or baby sister—things which someone else wrote and which he himself cannot now mean. It should always be remembered that children generally lack the adults' option of staying away when a ritual marks an event of which they disapprove.

The need for honesty in ritual expression is one which will come up again and again in the discussion to follow. It is true that ritual can shape our attitudes after the pattern of Christ. It does this, however, not by imputing feelings to us which we do not feel, but by engaging us in actions we might not spontaneously perform. By the act of giving thanks we may learn the attitude of gratefulness; by the act of confession we may broaden our conscience. As long as the prayer is focused on the gifts and grace of God, it will be appropriate for us regardless of our current state of mind, and therefore be all the more likely to draw us in and shape us to an honest and heartfelt response.

THE NEED TO BOND COMMUNITY

While some of our day-to-day ritualizations merely organize our individual lives, many of them function to regulate social interaction and reinforce social bonding. The handshake and other rituals of greetings, the formalized responses to certain verbal cues, all are part of the glue that holds society together. The same is true on a grander scale of the formal rituals of social groups. Following Durkheim, many sociologists and anthropologists have seen social bonding as the central purpose of religious and civil ritual. Shared symbols and shared action focused on those symbols bond a community together through both the appearance and the experience of acting as one.

We are social animals and we need community. There is a wide range of normalcy, from the gregarious type to the lover of solitude, but everyone needs a web of social connection, even if it only exists in their memory and in the representations they internalized based on the social world of childhood. Coming to a sense of personal identity can be a struggle against social pressures, but it cannot be achieved at all apart from a social context for identity, the range of symbolic choices held out to us by those around us. Most facets of our identity mark us as belonging to some group which shares that identifying characteristic: woman, Lutheran, American. In addition to identity, the communities we belong to supply us with the cognitive home of a shared world view, and the emotional home of a group of people who will recognize, support, and accept us.

Many people join congregations explicitly to find a community, a "church home." This has become more and more important a motivation in our mobile, urban society, where people often do not have family or longtime friends in town, and where there are not many built-in opportunities to form community. It is a need that many congregations are trying to meet through community-building activities and programs. Unfortunately, the sacramental and worship life of the church is not always recognized as the primary place to build community. A congregation may form geographical "clusters" or plan elaborate social events and never consider how its ritual life contributes to community. What does it mean that people are initiated into the community in private services with only the immediate family present? Why does this congregation celebrate the eucharist, which Augustine called "the sacrament of unity and love," only four times a year? There is no sharp line between the ritual and "social" life of the church, and a question such as how people leave the service (whether they are greeted and by whom, whether there is a "coffee hour") is a question of ritual as well as social practice. The point intended here is not an opposition between ritual and nonritual dimensions of community-making, but rather a reminder that whatever else we do together, the core of our communal identity is enacted in worship.

If the criterion for ritual practice arising from the concern for meaning is honesty, the pastoral imperative related to the concern for community is participation. The more widely and actively people participate in a ritual, the more they experience it as their own, as part of their identity, and the more connected they tend to feel with the other participants. At one extreme is the congregation where the people go to church to hear the pastor talk, perhaps saying amen now and then or joining in a chorus or two. At the other end of the spectrum is a community which corporately performs this "work of the people," singing all the hymns and liturgical songs, praying for each other's petitions, sharing the peace, taking turns as lectors, assistant ministers, or acolytes, baking the bread, making the vestments, paraments, banners, Advent wreath, and even the paschal candle, carrying the bread and wine from the community meal out to the homebound, hospitalized, and imprisoned. The pastoral way to increase community bonding through ritual is not primarily to "put on" inspiring ritual performances which will draw the people together as an audience, but to draw them into the task of celebrating the liturgy, of creating anew in this place the ancient rituals that bind the whole church of God.

THE NEED TO HANDLE
AMBIVALENCE

One of the greatest threats to order, meaning, and community in human life is the disruptive effect of ambivalent feelings. I use the term "ambivalent" here not in the colloquial sense of confused or vacillating, but in the psychoanalytic sense of opposite or conflicting. Our love can be shadowed by jealousy, our caring by resentment, our respect by envy, our sympathy by disdain. These emotional conflicts are never entirely overcome; they are part and parcel of the human condition. Theologically speaking, my contention is that ambivalence is not in and of itself sin, but rather a part of the created complexity of the human psyche. There are plenty of indications in nature that the Creator is fond of intricacy! To the extent that our freedom is grounded in our psychic complexity, the ambivalence is a condition of freedom and thus an occasion for sin and goodness alike. Whether ambivalence is understood as created intricacy or as itself a moral flaw, however, it is inarguably a challenge to the stability of relationships and the coherence of meaning.

Simpler animals use ritualized interactions to convey their roles and coming course of action clearly to each other, in order to keep from triggering an aggressive response, say, when the goal is to mate. Erik Erikson draws a parallel between this function of animal ritualization and the more complex function of human ritualization. As animals' ritualizations are developed to overcome ambiguity, Erikson proposes, so human ritualization is designed to overcome ambivalence (in addition to ambiguity).[2] Animal ritualization clarifies the behavioral message to avoid the arousal of conflicting instinctive responses, as in humans, it has been said, the extended open hand fends off the instinctual defensive response to a stranger's approach. Human ritualizations go beyond mere clarification of meaning, however, to an emotional reassurance which overcomes the conflicting feelings that arise even within clearly defined relationships.

There are two ways in which ritualization helps us to handle ambivalence. The first is by reinforcement of the preferred emotion; the second is by contained expression of the unwanted, conflicting emotion. (The preferred emotion in our cases will be the "positive" one, but some rituals are meant to reinforce seemingly "negative" feelings, such as hatred for the enemy.) The reinforcement of the intended feeling is done by lifting out of the interaction some element (a caress, a nickname, a word of thanks) which symbolizes that feeling and repeating it in an expectable pattern, possibly exaggerating it to enhance the emotional tone. The effect of this regular, symbolic repetition is to invest what was an unpredictable, intermittent element of the interaction with the experienced feel of constancy. I may feel many things toward you and you toward me, but this—the caring in this touch, the gratitude in this word—this is what you can count on, this is what is there again and again, this is what will always be there underneath. Out of the many conflicting feelings of human interaction, ritualization declares one set of attitudes to be continuous, reliable, perduring through all apparent interruptions.

The second ritual method for handling ambivalence is to provide a safe mode of expression for the conflicting emotions. This method is dependent upon the first, for expressing negative feelings can only be safe against the backdrop of the ritually established continuity of the positive. A primal example of such a ritually safe expression of negativity is peek-a-boo, where the fear and threat of disappearance or abandonment are playfully expressed in a secure context. The experience of "absence" is carefully contained within a ritual context of assured reappearance, accompanied by the repeated word. The empathic parent can sense how long to wait, so that the baby's trust is not stretched to the breaking point, and anxiety is contained in playful reassurance. Another example of this sort of ritualization, which is used at all ages, is teasing. Teasing is successful in this sense when it expresses envy (*not* disdain!) within a context of humorous affection. A "roast-and-toast" ceremony combines both the first and second methods, ritually emphasizing the positive and channeling the negative through humor.

The rituals of our churches, like most formal ceremony, use the first method of dealing with ambivalence extensively, emphasizing and reaffirming the appropriate emotional attitudes. They are less successful at providing occasions to express conflicting emotions. Based on psychological considerations alone, an important pastoral goal in ritual practice would be to let ritual encompass a range of human emotional response at the same time that it reaffirms the basic attitudes of faith. This can be achieved without subjectivizing. Ritual should not impute feelings, but it can allow symbolic room for feelings, by making recourse to a wider range of traditional models for speaking with God. We can give thanks and beg mercy, but we can also bargain with God like Abraham, mourn like Rachel, protest like Job, press our case beyond a dismissal like the Syrophoenician woman, or cry out of our abandonment like Jesus. A liturgical practice springing from biblical roots can certainly voice lament along with praise.[3] Yet despite the theological and psychological reasons for encompassing a wider range of feelings in ritual, many of our rites are unrelentingly positive in tone, univocal ceremonies of the pious attitude.

Transitions, for example, are times of much ambivalence, yet our rites of passage often mention only the positive, hopeful, forward-looking aspects of change. One retirement blessing I read recently spoke only of starting a new life, at a time when many people feel more loss than expectation. Even worse, some contemporary funerals, in an attempt to replace the black crepe of the past with an emphasis on resurrection hope, have managed to suppress all grief and protest. This may be acceptable at the funeral of a person who lived a long, full life and died a peaceful death, but when the death was untimely, tragic, or violent the funeral must say something in addition to alleluia. If the family of a young victim of a drunk driver, still in shock, requests Easter hymns and a celebration of the child's life, careful pastoral practice would indicate some ritual acknowledgment of the tragic nature of the death. Even when death does not come as a shock, there is generally loss, guilt, and anger alongside gratitude for the past and Christian hope for the future. We can learn a lesson in pastoral ritual from the Russian Orthodox, who have a two-part ritual for the dead: an evening service of mourning and eulogy followed by a vigil, and a morning mass of the resurrection. The idea is not that the family is expected to work through their grief in one night, but rather that loss and hope are held together in the church's ritual embrace. We need to find equivalent ways in our ritual to make room for the whole range of our response to God in the events of our lives. In theological terms, we need to remember that biblical faith is not defined by suppressing one's doubt and protest, but by addressing one's trust and doubt and praise and protest to God as if it mattered supremely to do so.

THE NEED TO ENCOUNTER MYSTERY

The earliest social ritualization of human life is the greeting ritual between the infant and the one who mothers her. The mutual recognition, the repeated naming, tone, and gestures, overcome the threat of separation with the reaffirmed continuity of the life-sustaining relationship. Here, according to Erik Erikson, is the developmental root of the "numinous" element of adult social ritual. The tiny child feels herself utterly dependent on this greater one who lifts her up in a safe embrace, recognizes her and names her, smiles upon her and gives her peace. The numinous, says Erikson, "assures us of separateness transcended and yet also of a distinctiveness confirmed, and thus of the very basis of a sense of 'I.'"[4] It becomes a quality of human social ritualization throughout life, this mutual recognition, this appeal to a greater reality—sometimes projected upon delusional visions in misplaced adulation, sometimes lived out in a healthy, shared, renewing faith. In religious ritual, of course, this element of the numinous is most clearly seen.

Unfortunately, we are often not very skilled at expressing the numinous in our religious ritual. It is a difficult thing to do: to speak of something which, though far beyond our experience, is yet in relation to us. The tension between awe and trust, so vividly evoked in Erikson's description of the infant in its mother's arms, is easily lost with our image of God receding into distant grandeur or settling into pedestrian familiarity. The difficulty of expressing the transcendent is inherent in the task, not specific to our culture, but our secular culture may find it harder than most.

The objection of Victor Turner and some other anthropologists to the last decades' liturgical renewal in the Roman Catholic church is that, in their opinion, the quality of transcendence was lost. Many Roman Catholics felt that in the move to the vernacular a sense of grandeur and mystery was forfeited. Indeed, in the early years of liturgical change, the concern for restoring a sense of community and relating the liturgy to the contemporary world often did take precedence over the expression of mystery and awesomeness. The language was not only English rather than Latin, it was often pedestrian in syntax, not evocative or richly symbolic. The songs were not only played on guitars rather than organs, they were often musically boring and simplistic. As the liturgical movement has matured, it has struggled to create liturgies which speak of mystery as well as community. The writers, having given up the crutch of archaism (thees and thous) to express transcendence, are searching for a liturgical syntax which is contemporary without being pedestrian, special without being quaint.

I once heard a theologian ridicule the new liturgy by extolling the old response to "The Lord be with you," "And with thy spirit," and lampooning the new response as "You too." In mourning the grandeur of the traditional response, this man overlooked two facts. First, the new response is not "You too" but "And also with you," which is in fact liturgical syntax, a special way of speaking, not something one would say to someone who said "Have a nice day." Second, the very distance of the traditional response from contemporary syntax led to an almost universal misunderstanding. Nearly everyone thought that the "spirit" referred to was not the minister's spirit but the Holy Spirit; thinking this, they missed the meaning of the action in which they were participating, that is, returning the minister's greeting. This illustrates the danger of clinging to grand-sounding traditional words when they have devolved from mystery into incomprehensibility. It also illustrates the challenge of finding special, holy words which are truly our own.

The need to express awe in ritual can sometimes seem to be at odds with the need to bond community. Theologically speaking, there cannot be any fundamental opposition, as the liturgical celebration of our common baptismal life is a celebration of both the heart of grace and the tie that binds. Pragmatically, however, the emphases on the "vertical" dimension of awe-filled worship and on the "horizontal" dimension of warm community often seem to counteract each other. It is important never to sacrifice the one to the other entirely, as both are fundamental ritual needs. They exist in different proportions in different individuals, but both needs are present in everyone in some form. My father loves the glory of Russian Orthodox liturgy and is quite ill at ease when asked to sit in a circle holding hands in silent prayer. Yet however justly he despises the "warm fuzzy" theory of liturgy, the community of the church in worship has unquestionably been a central focus of his identity and energy. The challenge for the liturgist is to respect the various admixtures of ritual needs found in different individuals and to gather all these people together with one Mystery at their center.

THE SACRAMENTS

The Mystery at the center of Christian community is ritually focused in the sacraments. All liturgy is a two-way street where God's action and human action meet, as our duty is caught up in God's gift and our gathering invested with God's presence. In the sacraments especially, the awareness that "God is doing something here" overwhelms us with grace, the core of the mystery of God's relation to us. Any discussion of the church's ritual must begin with the sacraments, particularly a discussion of pastoral meanings in ritual practice. As this book is not a work of systematic theology, nor meant to be a "confessional" book solely for those of a certain denominational tradition, I will keep my comments on the sacraments fairly general and not discuss them at a length proportionate to their importance. I hope in this section primarily to suggest some implications of the sacraments' centrality for the ritual life of the church. I will discuss here only the two "necessary" sacraments, baptism and the eucharist; other rites accepted as sacraments by some will come up later in other contexts.

Baptism

Baptism is the foundation of Christian life, Christian community, and ecumenism. The ground of our identity as Christians, baptism establishes that identity by incorporating us individually into the body of Christ, which includes both the local community that stands surety for us and the worldwide church born of the same waters. All worship is a celebration of our common baptism, for it is a corporate enactment of our identity as those united in the death and resurrection of Christ. All of life—worship, play, and work—is a living out of that same baptismal identity, the holy vocation, the "priesthood," that all Christians share.

The ritual practice of baptism in our churches has tended to skew the meaning of the act in two ways. First, we have obscured the lifelong importance of baptism by limiting its significance to a certain stage of the life cycle. In most of the liturgically minded churches, the children of members are baptized in infancy, and the danger is that baptism is relegated to the status of a life-cycle rite for babies. It becomes a "christening" in the popular sense of that word, a naming party. Its significance becomes so restricted to infancy that it seems awkward and inappropriate when older people are baptized. For one thing, they already have names; for another, their size is all out of proportion to the birdbath fonts. In churches which baptize most of their members' children in late childhood or adolescence, a similar limitation of significance can take place, only to a different point in the life cycle. Baptism can become the life-cycle rite of adolescence, the rite of passage to adulthood. "The day I accepted Jesus" can become as much a thing of one's personal past as "the day I was christened." Though a necessary prerequisite to being a Christian today, the event can have as little continuing significance as the math Scholastic Achievement Test has to a humanities major.

Whether the church baptizes mainly infants or adolescents, it is equally likely to fall into the second common distortion of baptism's meaning in ritual practice, that of privatization. Babies have often been baptized in private ceremonies on Sunday afternoons or even in the family home. The event is thus ritually stated to be of significance only to the immediate family and godparents. The wider communal meaning of baptism as incorporation into the whole body of Christ is obscured, replaced by the narrower one of the family's naming party. The privatization of "believer's baptism" takes place in a different way. The focus is not on the family so much as on the individual young person and his own inner experience of grace and decision. The emphasis on conscious commitment and personal responsibility is, of course, intentional, but this concentrated focus often blurs the larger picture, the corporate nature of life and faith in the community of the baptized.

Many of the efforts of the liturgical movement have been directed at reestablishing in ritual practice the lifelong centrality and corporate meaning of baptism. First and foremost, there has been a move toward a fuller celebration of the rite of baptism itself. There was much symbolic richness in the early Christian rite of initiation: the fonts large enough to suggest baths or tombs, the candles and new robes, the oil of priestly and royal anointing. The recovery of some of this symbolic richness can emphasize the importance of baptism and dramatize the fact that baptism has enough layers of meaning to last a lifetime. The renewed attention to adult baptism following the implementation of the Roman Catholic "Rite of Christian Initiation of Adults" has also helped to demonstrate the seriousness of baptism, which is important enough to demand extensive preparation of adults, even as the new fonts are big enough to receive them. A fuller celebration of baptism also means an intentionally communal one. More and more, baptisms are celebrated at the regular worship service in the presence of the whole community; some rites have the community actively participate by joining in the credal responses. There are a variety of ways ritually to underline the corporate dimension of the event. One pastor I know takes the infant from its parents or godparents after the prayers and carries it into the middle of the congregation to "present" it to the community. In doing this, she emphasizes that this child is now a responsibility of—and a gift to—the whole community, not just the immediate family. In a Hispanic church I visited, the baptismal party processed down the aisle and people from the congregation came up to sign the baby's forehead with the sign of the cross.

There are other ways the liturgical movement has re-emphasized the centrality of baptism and its corporate nature, outside the actual performance of the rite itself. Prime among these is the recovery of the Easter Vigil as the queen of feasts, the celebration from which and to which all Christian liturgy flows. The Vigil demonstrates the centrality and communality of baptism as no other ritual can for it remembers the death and resurrection of Christ *through* remembering our common baptism into that mystery. The readings speak of Easter through baptismal references to the flood or the Red Sea or the Spirit enlivening bones. The font is the focus of the whole community, recognized as the community's present entry into the mystery of cross and resurrection. In celebrating the Easter Vigil we know baptism as the core of our Christian identity, individually and corporately alike.

Clearer links are also being made between baptism and subsequent rites of first communion or confirmation, in order to keep these rites from becoming important in people's minds at baptism's expense. Instead, it is emphasized that the importance of these rites is derived from baptism and is a further explication of what baptism itself entails. Communion is the birthright of the baptized, not the reward for catechetical drill, even if it does not follow directly on baptism. Confirmation is an important "affirmation of baptism," but it is baptism and not confirmation that makes one a member of Christ's church.

Finally, the reawakened emphasis on baptism has found its way into the week-to-week ritual practice of many communities in a great variety of forms. To do ritual justice to baptism as the ever-flowing fount of our corporate life, there must be constant reminders of baptism spread throughout our liturgy. The sign of the cross, the creed, the aspergus, all can be connected more explicitly to baptism. The font can be placed so that people have to walk by or around it to get into the church, physically reminding them that we enter into God's community by way of our baptism. Baptismal anniversaries can be remembered in the prayers or marked in other ways. One Sunday School posts baptismal anniversaries each week on the bulletin board and celebrates them in class. Baptismal candles are conducive to such celebrations and can be given to those who didn't get them at baptism—perhaps at the Vigil. The general confession can, in the spirit of the Reformation, be announced as a return to the grace of baptism. Eventually the sheer repetition will have its effect. One seminarian spent his internship year making constant references to baptism in ritual and preaching; at the end of the year he was rewarded by someone's spontaneous suggestion that the Sunday School should send the children not birthday cards but baptism-day cards. A good example of a spontaneous ritualization of Christian identity!

The Eucharist

If baptism is the core of Christian identity, the eucharist is the central continuing enactment of that identity. It is the banquet for which we received the festal robe, the family meal to which our adoption entitles us. In it, we as the people of God exercise the priestly function to which we were anointed, offering to God our liturgical remembrance of what God has offered us. In bread and wine we taste the life won for us on the cross, the same cross that was originally and enduringly marked on us in our baptism. We know that life as our possession individually—as the Lutherans say to each person in the distribution, "given for you"—and also corporately, in the most fundamental communal act of sharing a meal.

As it is, only Disciples of Christ, Episcopalians, the Orthodox, Roman Catholics and a smattering of others celebrate this fundamental Christian ritual weekly. Resistance to the frequent celebration of communion can derive from many factors, from the "sixty-minute mentality" to an attachment to a congregation's traditional practice to the contention that familiarity breeds contempt. (A friend of mine combats this last argument with the analogy of making love to one's spouse; don't do it too often, he cautions ironically, or it won't be "special" anymore. Four times a year, tops.) One factor which I would contend often plays a role in such resistance is the ritual poverty of the celebration to which most people are accustomed. A child of my acquaintance approached her first communion with great excitement, anticipating the wonders of "God's bread"; when she tasted the sticky, papery wafer she said, softly but distinctly, "Yucky." Luckily her family was able to convey to her the importance and wonder of the meal in a way that survived her encounter with wafers. The point here is that a fuller, more richly and adequately symbolic celebration of the eucharist is the best argument for greater frequency.

The liturgical movement has initiated a number of changes in this direction. The most well-known is the rediscovery of the predominantly communal nature of the ritual, which had been obscured by the individualistic piety of rosary-telling Catholics and head-bowing Protestants alike. The symbolism of the community's gathering around a table has been restored as far as possible, both architecturally and in ritual word and action. The increased participation of laypeople in many churches is itself a symbol of the eucharist's communal nature. A single loaf of real bread baked by a member of the community is a richer and more adequate symbol in a score of ways than a pile of anonymous stamped-out wafers or cubes of store-bought bread, and its symbolic power is only intensified if for many people it is the only fresh-baked, homemade bread they ever eat. We who are many are one, for we eat of the one loaf. The more our symbolic expression is adequate to the richness of the meaning in this sacrament, the more likely it is that people will catch a whiff of that meaning, like the smell of fresh bread, and be drawn to the table.

As the eucharist is the central enactment of Christian community, it is extremely important to be aware of the effect on those who are excluded from participation. The major category here is, of course, the young children. If it is decided on theological ground to delay the communing of baptized children some years, there should be careful pastoral attention to the way in which that delay is explained to the children. There is no truly effective way to convey what the liturgical scholars would like to emphasize, that communion is one's birthright by baptism, even if delayed. If you've ever tried to explain to a five-year-old that a gift of money is really his when you've banked it for him, you know what a lost cause this argument would be. There are, though, more and less pastoral ways to handle this exclusion. Giving children a baptismal blessing at the communion rail may remind them of their rightful place within the community. If little children take the opportunity to reach for the bread or cup, this does not necessarily mean that they will feel the denial any more acutely than they would if left sitting in the pew. It does mean, however, that now the adults have to deal with the child's expressed desire to be fed. The most cowardly response I've seen to this uncomfortable situation was a bulletin item which read: "During communion children may come with their parents for a blessing. Noncommuning children should not extend their hands." This seems to be serving the adults' need at the expense of the child. To spare themselves the confusion and discomfort of refusing a direct request, the grownups have placed the onus on the child, who is told that expressing an untoward desire for God's bread is misbehaving. If we are going to exclude some of the baptized from God's table, we can at least refrain from ritually telling them that their hunger is bad.

It is often assumed that children accept the idea that communion is for older folks and so do not feel excluded. Perhaps this is true for some children, though understanding that children are not allowed to do certain things isn't generally proof against their feeling left out. In any case, I have heard many stories like the following:

A two-year-old girl went up to the altar with her mother, who received communion. As they walked back down the aisle, the child asked, "What are you eating?"

"I'm eating the body of Christ."

"Can I have some?"

"No, I'm sorry, you can't have it. You'll have to wait till you're a big girl."

As soon as they got home from church, the child went to the kitchen and took down the box of Triscuits, walked to the dining room and took a silver bowl out of the china cabinet, placed some crackers in the bowl, and took them into her father's study. "Look, Daddy, I have some body of Christ." The father innocently asked, "Can I have some?"—to which the girl responded emphatically, "No, this is just for little girls." Though this child dealt with the feeling of exclusion creatively, by turning the tables in play, the hurt of being left out was clearly there, inspiring the dramatized revenge. Rather than making the comfortable assumption that children don't mind being denied communion, we need to pay more attention to the ritual needs of the nonparticipant. This child's story also demonstrates a more general phenomenon we need always to keep in mind: the unexpectedly powerful psychological effects of taken-for-granted ritual practice.

LIFE-CYCLE RITUAL

In another book in this series, *Life-Cycle Theory and Pastoral Care*, Donald Capps discusses the work of Erik Erikson on the life cycle, and in one section treats the role of the pastor as "ritual coordinator," one who integrates the various ritual processes which shape the community's life. Capps concentrates in this section primarily on the ritualization of everyday life, the semi-formalized customs which regulate the church's activity. Like Capps, I will be working here from a psychological perspective based on Erikson's work. Not wishing to go over ground Capps has covered well, I will neither review Erikson's theory nor treat the ritualization concerns of each stage of life. Instead, in the discussion which follows I will focus on the formal rites attached to the various phases and transitions of the life cycle. Rather than discussing them one by one, I will raise questions which are relevant to the whole spectrum of life-cycle rites in practice.

The rites which function at least in part as life-cycle rituals in the church are a mixed bag. They include sacraments which usually fall at certain ages, nonsacramental rites such as Protestant confirmation, church addenda to secular events, such as the baccalaureate, and occasional services such as house blessings. The expected pattern of life-cycle ritual may include infant baptism, first communion in mid-childhood, confirmation in early adolescence, baccalaureates for high school and college graduations, marriage, the baptisms of one's children, blessings on major anniversaries and at retirement, and the rite for the dying. In addition, there are rituals marking events which come in no set sequence but which mark significant transitions in individuals' lives, such as occasional services for moves or new jobs, or the funerals of one's relatives and friends,

Other rites which have been advocated recently include some sort of non-familial life-cycle rite for adults, celebrating vocation and/or mature faith commitment, and a ritual for the divorcing couple or family. The very proposal of these rites raises complicated questions of ritual's relation to the "normative Christian life," and will be discussed in that light below.

The Need for Life-Cycle Rites

The understanding of the function of life-cycle rites grew out of anthropologists' study of pubertal initiation rites in traditional cultures. The rite marking the transition from childhood to adulthood is the paradigmatic "rite of passage"—a phrase coined by Arnold van Gennep.[5] Van Gennep was the first to recognize the common dynamic operating in various rites which accompany a passage from one social status or group to another, such as rites of birth, initiation, and marriage. All such rites, says van Gennep, include three phases: separation from the old status, transition, and incorporation into the new status. Victor Turner has expanded on van Gennep's scheme with emphasis on the culture's handling of the liminal state, the fuzzy middle ground of transition.[6] Change in an individual's life is a potential threat to the whole social group, which knows how to treat someone who is in a clearly defined state but not someone who hovers between states. To regularize the transitions and include them also in the ritually defined world of meaning, rites of passage were developed to midwife the individual's birth into a new social status. Is this girl a child or an adult? Can she be married? The rite of passage both affects and clarifies the change in social status, regularizing a confusingly gradual and idiosyncratic biological process and letting one know how to behave toward one's neighbors.

The individual psychological aspect of this is that we all derive our self-definitions, more or less creatively, from society's definitions of us. It is personally disturbing not to know whether one is "really" a child or an adult, whether a relationship is committed or not. Society may need rites of passage to realign and clarify the interactions between people in different stages and conditions, but the individual also needs help in making it out of an outgrown state of being, through the dangerous anomic period of liminality, and into a state of being where he knows who he has become and what he can now do.

The work of Turner and others on rites of passage has motivated within the church both a renewed attention to the pastoral needs of people in transition and an attempt to revitalize and extend the church's ritual structure to meet such needs. Some people have seen this as an argument for the placing of sacraments and parasacramental rites at points of transition in the life cycle. They might advise, for example, having first communion at the onset of school or the close of grade school, or delaying confirmation until the "real" beginning of adult Christian life (whenever that may be). Others have created or revived occasional rites for other transitions, such as moving or retiring.

It is possible, however, to go overboard, with unrealistic expectations about the church's ability to help people negotiate their social passages. Some years back, Margaret Mead was acting as an advisor to an Episcopalian committee studying these questions. When they suggested that young people need a rite of passage into adulthood, Mead concurred, but added that the American teenager for whom the church could supply such a rite would be a pretty strange kid. Her point was that the hallmarks of adulthood in our culture are not negotiated by the church, but by the schools, the government, and other social structures. The turning points are high school and college graduation, or the various ages at which one is legally allowed to drive, to buy alcohol, and to vote, or required to register for the draft. The church cannot make a ritual meaningful simply by creating it to fit some preconceived notion of people's ritual needs.

The best plan is to listen to what people say about the turning points in their lives. What are the important transitions? Which of them would they like the church to take official notice of, to ritualize in some way? Would they like major wedding anniversaries acknowledged or new homes blessed? If the transition is one that is secularly defined, like getting a driver's license, there may be ways for the church to "solemnize" the event. In one congregation teenagers are ritually handed their car keys in church, with a blessing and prayers for responsibility and safety. A community could try out ritualizations of various events and see which ones "take." People may not know whether they'd appreciate a ritual for a given occasion until they've experienced it. One young, single pastor held a house blessing party at his new house and invited the "singles" group. They came diffident and most were swayed by the experience; there was something satisfying about blessing a single person's house as a home holy in God's eyes. For a community that is ready to experiment with ritualiz-

ing more aspects of its members' lives, the new books of occasional services put out by the Episcopalians and the Lutherans are good resources, as
is the less formal but wider-ranging book, *Blessings for God's People.*[7] Then,
after trying new rituals for a while, the pastoral task is to ask and to listen.
What had meaning for you? Did the ritual change your experience of the
event or transition it marked? How did you feel about rituals designed for
others that didn't include you? What rites would include you and your
ritual needs?

Sacraments as Life-Cycle Rites

While many American liturgical workers have been excited about the
potential for the church to ritualize our passages, Europeans have tended
to be more suspicious of the life-cycle functions of church ritual. This is
due to their experience of the state church, where the church took over
social ritual functions to the extent that there may have been no other way
to get married, say, than in the church. Rather than christianizing society,
this merger of ritual function ended up secularizing the rites of the church,
reducing their meaning in people's minds to a socially expected life-cycle
rite and nothing more. Baptism, administered automatically to everyone
except Jews, became a naming ritual, a "christening." One American
Methodist minister was astonished by the requests for baptism he heard
during his time working in England: "I'd like my baby done tomorrow."
When he tried to explain to one woman that Methodists don't baptize
without some assurance that the child will be associated with the church,
the perplexed mother responded, "But what will we call him then?" The
Europeans have reason to be wary of this devaluation of the sacraments
into generic life-cycle rites. They have seen the rituals of the church co-
opted by the secular society, and in reaction they often want the church to
draw clear lines of separation between its own proper sacramental work
and the society's ritualization of the life cycle.

This secular co-opting of the church's liturgy is not quite so much a
problem in the United States, thanks to the separation between church
and state. It does still happen here, though, in a less systemic fashion.
People want their children baptized due to social or familial expectations
rather than a wish to bring them up in the church. Couples want to get
married in church because it is "traditional" and a lovely setting. Now,
one should not be too quick to judge such people and discount their
motives as merely secular. For some of them, there may be a genuine sense

of touching on the numinous in times of transition, or at least a wish for cosmic reassurance arising out of the insecurity of liminality. This religious need may be none the less genuine for all its being situation-specific and having no perceptible aftereffects. Even given this generous evaluation of motives, however, a genuinely religious need does not necessarily constitute a readiness for making the Christian commitment called for by the church's rite.

As this issue here is the meaning of the church's rite, we must return to the criterion of honesty. Will the participants mean what the ritual says? Will the church mean what it says in relation to them? These are not simple questions, in part because there is no foolproof way to predict the future. Some people push in favor of preserving the integrity of the sacraments and advocate stricter guidelines for, say, administering infant baptism. Others tend to give the ones who ask the benefit of the doubt, not wanting to stifle their inchoate religious needs and alienate them from the church for good. Sometimes it is possible to solve this by creating a ritual alternative to the church's sacrament, to meet the person's ritual need without compromising the integrity of the core Christian symbols. Some communities, for instance, have a form for blessing babies whose parents are not committed enough to warrant baptism (this is different from the infant dedication practiced in some churches with believer's baptism, where the assumption usually is that the child will be brought up in the church). The Episcopal *Book of Occasional Services* has a form for the burial of "one who does not profess the Christian faith." Such rituals risk causing some confusion in people's minds, but they may allow the church to respond both positively and honestly to the ritual needs of non-members.

As long as some level of honesty is maintained, there is no problem with sacraments' serving in part as life-cycle rites. Van Gennep himself insisted that none of the rituals he described was *merely* a rite of passage: marital ceremonies may also include fertility rites, birth ceremonies may involve rites of protection, etc.[8] The danger that the church's rituals will devolve in people's minds into "mere" rites of passage simply points to the need for pastoral care in the area of liturgical education. The suggestions made earlier in regard to making baptism a continual focus of community life constitute a project in liturgical education; such a project must go far beyond verbal explanations to pervade the whole worship life of the community with ritual reminders of its sacramental core.

The Conversion/Nurture Question

The worry that sacraments will devolve into mere life-cycle rites is related to the traditional debate over conversion vs. nurture in the making of Christians. This educational and theological debate bears on questions of ritual practice whenever the discussion focuses on rites of initiation or commitment to the faith. People who want the theological and ritual emphasis placed squarely on the necessity of conversion and intentional commitment will argue for a practice of believer's baptism, adult baptism, or some rite of adult commitment for those baptized in infancy. Others, while recognizing the indispensability of personal commitment, feel that there are problems with trying to identify and ritualize this element of Christian identity, and see ritual primarily as a means of incorporating individuals into the body of believers and nurturing the possibility of faith.

The lines of debate which can seem clearly drawn in ideology often blur in practice. I have a friend from a believer's-baptism church who was baptized at the age of seven. In an article in *Liturgy*, Glenn Hinson wrote with concern of "the precipitous downward plunge in the age for baptism" in Southern Baptist churches, attributing this in part to the nurturing program these churches have developed, and in part to the pressure applied by families and aggressive evangelists.[9] On the other hand, groups which rely more heavily on the corporate model of ritual care may still find themselves having to assess someone's level of personal commitment—if not that of the infant, then that of the parents who bring it for baptism. If the parents do not intend to bring the child to church, how can the community nurture it to faith? No matter where the emphasis is placed, every community has to deal with two facts: that they are, in fact, bringing children up in the church, and that faith does not come automatically in this process.

The life-cycle view used as a framework here may seem to accord better with an emphasis on nurture. Nonetheless, I do not mean to imply by the life-cycle language that everyone follows a chartable course of predictable growth in faith. There is no one pattern of becoming a Christian, when looked at from a psychological point of view. Some people experience one or more conversions and cannot imagine how anyone could be a real Christian without experiencing such a radical re-orientation. They understand their childhood Christianity to have been empty convention, awaiting a personal decision to give it existential meaning. Others experience their growth in faith as a continuity, a deepening and constant renewing of the very faith which permeated the air they breathed in childhood. These may not be "once-born" types in the Jamesian sense of rather shallow optimism; they may struggle just as much with the problem of evil but the struggle, like the conversion of heart, is for them a more gradual and ongoing process.

Our ritual patterns need to be flexible enough to allow for various modes of becoming a Christian. To some extent, certainly, it is denominational pluralism which provides this flexibility, so that people who seek a rebirth tend to gravitate toward groups which ritualize such experience. There can also, however, be a healthy pluralism within a community, and ritual can be a part of that. One way to encourage this is simply by increasing the number of occasions for ritualized expression of growth in faith. Many Roman Catholic parishes have found that using the RCIA in Lent when there are adults to be baptized has become an experience which revitalizes the whole community, drawing many members into a reexamination of their faith through their ritual participation in the catechetical process. Other adults have experienced a similar renewal by being drawn into the preparations for their child's (or godchild's) first communion, and being ritually involved in the event. Marriage encounter weekends often include ritual expressions of mutual commitment in faith. Courses of adolescent and adult Christian education can culminate in rituals which help draw the members beyond reading and discussion into a corporate experience of a new dimension of grace—as when a Lenten class on wholeness and salvation leads to a service of healing during Holy Week. Celebrations of vocation for adults, a ritually serious experience of being a godparent, the investiture of laypeople as bringers of communion to the housebound: all such events are ritual occasions for growth in faith, which the individual can appropriate to express and articulate her own unique pattern of birth and rebirth, of struggle and turnaround or steady unfolding.

There has been a good deal of talk in liturgical circles about the "norm of adult baptism." This means various things to various people. To some, it means that the ritual initiation of adults should be recognized as the normative way of making Christians. These people have rediscovered the power, vitality, and integrity of the ancient ritual sequence of catechesis, initiation, and mystagogy and see in its revival the hope for a renewed church. Ideally, they think, it should become statistically normative, the most common way of ritually entering the church—a basically Baptist solution, though arrived at by some rather un-Baptist arguments of liturgical form and ritual integrity. Failing that, it should at least be acknowledged that the general practice of baptizing infants is an extraordinary waiver of the assumed requirement, an exception to the rule which remains an exception no matter how commonly done and justified only by the firm commitment of the parents and solid assurance that the child will be brought up in the church.

What this position ignores is the fact that there are *two* liturgical witnesses to be heard from. The first witness is the ancient form of ritual preparation, initiation, and integration, which demonstrates what a serious and demanding business it is to take on a Christian identity. The second witness, as Thomas Droege has pointed out, is the pastoral wisdom of the church's ritual nurture of its own children, a wisdom which has developed over centuries of practice.[10] In this light the spreading-out of the initiatory rites over the course of childhood and adolescence need not be seen as a devolution of the pristine integrity of the unitary rite of initiation, but as a pastoral response to the developmental process of growing into one's Christian identity within the church. The rediscovery of the first witness does not have to make us discount the developmental wisdom of the practice which has become traditional. What it can and should do is impel us to find ways through education and ritual experience to embody the power and awesome seriousness of the ancient initiatory rite. Much of the work at reviving the Easter Vigil, the catechetical meaning of Lent, and the connection between baptism and the Vigil has served to lead us in this direction.

The church always has two pastoral concerns in the nurture of its children: to give them from the start a world in which the perspective of faith is taken for granted, and to help them as they grow to internalize that perspective and appropriate it as their own deepest commitment. Ritual can help toward both ends. It can surround them with the symbols of faith, blessing the implicit process of growth. It can provide occasions for, and confirmation of, their individually emerging, intentional commitment to those symbols. The theological assumption here is that the sacraments and other ritual acts of the church are means of grace—that one grace which underlies and enables all our ways of coming to faith.

The criterion of honesty also applies to the conversion/nurture dimension of ritual meaning. Glenn Hinson describes seeing four-year-old twins dragged down the aisle in a Baptist church by their mother and promptly immersed along with the others "requesting" baptism.[11] These children were involved despite themselves in ritual dishonesty. So was I, when at the age of twelve I was told that I was making an adult, lifelong promise of fidelity to the Christian faith, up to and including martyrdom, and that I was doing this freely. I had no sense of choice and literally could not imagine how my parents would react if I decided not to be confirmed; it was simply not a thinkable contingency. Ritual honesty demands that we do not request lifelong commitments from people whom society does not consider (and who do not consider themselves) old enough to make such a commitment, that we do not pretend that participation in a rite is freely chosen when the individual will know himself constrained. This last is particularly a problem with children, who are seldom free to determine their level of religious involvement. There may be ways of alleviating the element of familial and peer pressure, as in a Presbyterian experiment of replacing "confirmation" with a four-year (high school) discipleship program, with an option for ritual expression of commitment each year. Since there was no longer a one-time standardized ceremony, the teens had more freedom to choose their expression of commitment. More efforts like this must be made to develop rites which nurture faith and provide the occasion for growth in commitment, without falling into the dishonest practice of enforcing the language of decision and choice.

Ritual and the
Normative Life Cycle

As was stated above in the section on the need for meaning, ritual's function of affirming the community's central meaning-structure carries with it an inevitable normative dimension. When rituals serve in part as life-cycle rites, this prescriptive force means that they are perceived as defining the normative Christian life cycle. In the ritual systems most of us grew up in, for instance, the only life-cycle rites provided for adults were familial ones: marriage, the baptism of one's children. The normative pattern implied by the ritual structure was baptism, confirmation, marriage, children, death. There was no rite designed specifically with the single adult lay Christian in mind. The ritual focus on marriage and families and on the ordained could be felt by single laypeople to have evaluative force, excluding them from the church's central concern and from the norm of Christian adulthood. It is to fill that gap, and to expand the ritual norm of the Christian life cycle, that various life-cycle rites for adults have recently been developed and urged.

One common suggestion is for rites blessing the Christian vocation of individual members. This has worked well in some communities.[12] One should, however, be careful not to identify vocation too directly with job, as that brings its own problems in the area of the church's norms over against societal norms. The society's value system says that what is paid is worthy, and what is paid more is worthier. It is crucial for a Christian celebration of vocation to hold up a different and broader vision of what is worth doing. The other problem of focusing on jobs *per se* is that the sense of vocation in one's job may be a function of economic privilege to the extent that the experience of choice and meaningfulness in relation to one's work is privileged. The normative force of ritual to exclude some from the ritually defined ideal would be all too evident if the professionals in the congregation got to celebrate their vocations and the intermittently employed or those on disability did not. It may be safe to celebrate aspects of vocation, rather than the unitary concept of "vocation," which is too easily equatable with job. One pastor I know approves of the expanded use of services of healing, but feels that the rites tend to treat people too passively, only as recipients of healing. He feels that there should also be recognition, confirmation, blessing of the ways in which we each bring God's healing to others. Such confirmation would be a celebration of Christian vocation that would not be confined by social definitions of role and occupation.

Another suggestion for a life-cycle rite for adults is a rite of adult commitment to the faith, designed for those who were baptized in infancy and brought up in the church. The problems here, of course, are those of setting the age and assessing the commitment. People who advocate such a rite generally set the appropriate age at around 30 or 35, either because they adhere to the upper-middle-class view of the 20s as extended adolescence or because they have read Jung. In a way, what they are attempting is to try to do honestly what confirmation claimed to do: catch people when they are really ready to make a lifelong commitment. The difficulty is that once again there is created a single norm of the Christian life cycle, according to which real commitment comes around 30. If only some church members fit this pattern and participate in the ritual, there is the danger of a two-tier membership, divided between the real adult Christians and the merely baptized (I would be tempted to stick with the merely baptized on principle!). One solution might be, as with adolescents, to provide repeated opportunities for such statements of intentional commitment, perhaps in the context of the Easter Vigil, or as an affirmation of baptism at the conclusion of some undertaking in spiritual growth, such as an adult class, a retreat, or a Lenten discipline. This would provide adults with new opportunities for the ritual expression and blessing of their maturing faith, without setting up the narrowly normative expectations of a once-for-all rite of adult commitment.

Ritual and Norms: A Rite for Divorce?

In interviewing a number of people on whether the church should provide a rite for the divorcing, I received from one pastor a succinct answer: "Pastorally, yes. Theologically, no." This pastor spoke out of an awareness of the inevitable normative dimension of ritual practice. Though he thinks that divorce is an important and difficult transition that calls out for a rite of passage, he is afraid that the church cannot provide a rite which would be both honest and helpful. Theologically, he thought, the ritual would have to say that there has been a failure to uphold the covenant of marriage as an icon of God's faithfulness—but saying that would hardly be a pastoral response to the people's current need and pain.[13]

Actually, the issue is even more complicated and conflictual than that. The prior problem is that there is not really *any* clear normative understanding of divorce on which to proceed. Some people see divorce as an unequivocally positive option when the couple "grows apart"; to be ritually honest, these people should (and sometimes do) modify their marriage vows to eliminate the promise of lifelong commitment. Some see divorce as tragedy or failure, arising from human finitude; some see it primarily as sin. And some see it as any one of the above (or a combination of the last two), depending on the circumstances of the individual divorce. Amid all this ambiguity, it is difficult for a church body to come up with a rite that will work for more than a small minority of its divorcing couples.

One way to investigate the ritual–norm relationship is to look at the different metaphors used in proposed rites of divorce and explore their normative and pastoral implications. In the rites I have seen or heard proposed, I have found four major metaphors or paradigms used to express the experience of divorce, the couple's need, and the church's response.

The first of these views divorce as freedom from a relationship that had become constraining, and the normative assumption is that it is therefore an unshadowed good. The rite printed in *Ritual in a New Day* uses this metaphor of freedom, speaking of the divorce as a kind of natural ebbtide in the "rhythm of union and separation" that is human relationship.[14] The unequivocally positive view of divorce here is precisely what many people fear when they say the church should not "celebrate" a divorce. In fact, the symbolic action in this rite reinforces the sense of celebration in a way that approaches a parody of the wedding, when the couple give each other their wedding rings "reconsecrated to your freedom."

The second paradigm used in some rites is that of repentance and grace, so that the ritual analogy is to confession and absolution.[15] While this takes seriously the moral dimension of the covenant broken, it raises complex pastoral issues. For one thing, while no one is ever guilt-free in any relationship, an abandoned spouse might be innocent with respect to the divorce. For another, even when both acknowledge the elements of moral responsibility and sin, it is questionable, pastorally speaking, to emphasize this in the rite or to single them out as sinners by virtue of their divorce. In most churches these days, there is no other situation where the church publicly draws attention to an individual member's sin. The divorce rites usually, in fact, try to offset this effect by adding some general congregational confession of sin and failures in faithfulness.

Partly in order to escape or balance the heavy moralization of the repentance paradigm, some rites have turned to the metaphor of death and resurrection. The "death" of the marriage, and of the hopes and dreams associated with that relationship, is acknowledged and mourned, and the "resurrection" of new life is prayed for.[16] It might be argued that the analogy of the funeral avoids the appearance of celebrating the event at the same time that it refrains from singling out the divorcing as public sinners. The problem, however, is in the application of the promise of resurrection to such a morally ambiguous "death." There is a promise attached to the death of a Christian, by virtue of her baptismal participation in Christ's passage to Easter, but is there a promise attached to the death of a commitment? No, in the sense that the commitment itself has no future beyond death; yes, in the sense that all our sins and failures are gathered up into the cross. The language of resurrection must be used carefully, that the Easter message not be devolved into a blithe promise of a fresh start.

The fourth paradigm is that of suffering and wholeness, according to which the ritual analogue and pattern would be a rite of healing.[17] The advantage of this pattern is that it allows for a healing also of guilt, for forgiveness, without focusing on the guilt and seeming to "rub it in." People who participate in the new rites of healing are often seeking a generalized healing of their brokenness, the forgiveness of sin as well as the alleviation of suffering. Thus the language of healing would be accessible to a wide range of divorcing individuals. If the congregation is used to the laying on of hands in rites of healing, it would seem natural and not forced to use it in this situation. In any case, the normative statement of God's will to heal suffering (including the suffering caused by sin) is one everyone can agree on.

What are the pastoral needs to consider in designing a rite of divorce? First, the man and woman need closure. They need to let go of the dead relationship and acknowledge its ending, to deal with the feelings this brings, to forgive the other. Almost any public ritual of divorce can help contribute to a sense of closure. Long descriptions of personal feelings to be resolved, however, should be kept to private rituals within a close circle of friends, and not inflicted on the congregation.[18] Second, they may sense a need for forgiveness, for their own fault or their bitterness toward the other. This could be handled privately through a rite of private confession and absolution or included among other themes in a public rite of healing at the individual's or couple's request. Third, there is the need for healing, of all the suffering and brokenness and division in the couple and among their children and families and friends (which may include most of the congregation). Fourth, the couple (if both are members) needs the community's acknowledgment of the divorce and pledge of support to them as individuals. Too often a congregation does not want to face the reality of a divorce and refuses to deal with it by refusing to deal with one or both spouses. One should not try to force the congregation to "affirm the couple's decision" by putting words in its mouth, but one might ask the assembly to acknowledge the divorce, to pledge mutual support within the Christian community, and to pray for healing. Fifth, the couple and their children need a definition of their new status after the divorce. This may involve such things as a recognition of a woman's change of name, or the altered but continuing commitment of a noncustodial parent to the children. Children always need assurance of both parents' continuing commitment to them, and this is one area where the church can give an unqualified blessing. (As was cautioned above, however, children should never be pressured into making ritual statements they may not be able to mean. If they want to write their own, fine.) Another "rite of incorporation" into a new status might be a house blessing of a newly constituted household, say, that of custodial parent and children. Such a family is called "broken" and usually feels a great gap in its emotional structure, and a home blessing might bring healing by recognizing the "wholeness" and blessedness of this family group in God's eyes. The house blessing could be adapted to make mention of the children's having a "second home" as well; that also is a fragmentation which could use a healing touch.

This discussion was meant to illustrate how pastoral and normative considerations combine in all questions of ritual care. The individual circumstances of divorces are quite different, and as with any public, communal ritual, the pastor must be sensitive to individuals' needs as well as to communal patterns. In the next chapter, the discussion will turn to ritual care focused more directly on individuals and individual families, in rites largely carried out in private rather than in the public assembly.

CHAPTER 2

Ritual and Care
for
the Individual

RITUAL AND INDIVIDUAL NEEDS

Many people who can concur with much of what has been said about ritual in community life will find themselves becoming skeptical as the focus turns to the individual. Ritual, they might think, is a kind of formalized interaction which is appropriate for community events, and which society developed to answer certain generic needs: the need to shape communal grief, for example, or to mark the passage into adulthood. More individualized needs seem to call for more personalized interactions.

This last statement is true: interactions more personalized than formal communal ritual are needed. Yet in some situations the personalized interaction needed may itself be a ritual. All ritual has formal elements and draws on the social group's symbolic world view rather than a purely private set of symbols. Given these attributes, however, there is a great variability among rituals in the degree of formalization. The fewer people involved, and the better they know one another's needs, the more flexibility and adaptation is possible within the limits of the ritual's meaning.

The conflict many people see between ritual and an empathic response to individual needs has often been created by poor pastoral practice. Ritual can indeed be used by pastors as a way of avoiding the particular, thorny human problem before them, by escaping into preset, pious formulas. The minister who prays with a person without first listening to her produces a prayer which bears only a chance relationship to her needs. He may even use the ritual to fend off her needs, by praying in such a way as to preclude any questions or "wrong" thoughts on her part. Such abuses of ritual do not, however, mean that ritual and empathy are antithetical.

This person's needs may well include a need for shared prayer, and the more the minister listens the better he will be able to tailor the ritual language to the individual situation.

The split between "ritualists" and "counselors" has gone so deep that, at the other extreme from the unempathic ritualist, one finds the minister who listens and listens and never prays. This may be appropriate in some situations (in long-term, intensive therapy, say, or with ritual-shy parishioners), but as a constant strategy it can be just as much a means of avoidance as unasked-for ritualizing. At worst, this strategy can also be used to fend off the other's need, by treating the request for prayer as a symptom to be interpreted away.

The apparent conflict, incarnate in poor pastoral practice at both extremes, is at heart a false dichotomy. Good pastoral practice involves both listening and praying, empathy and ritual. The pastor who does both well will be able to adapt rituals to individual situations, coming in prayer to meet the person's particular need. Once again, this adaptation does not imply that the felt need becomes the norm which determines the ritual statement; rather, listening to that need is the necessary first step to a two-way process. The church's symbols reach out to embrace an individual's inmost questions and longings. These questions and longings are in turn transformed by the symbol's evocation of a broader vision of God and a shared history of failure and forgiveness, of suffering, protest, and endurance, of forsakenness and blessing. The "why me" of the cancer patient is not foreclosed by falsely pious ritual, but neither is it simply enshrined, as is, in the form of prayer. It is placed into symbolic contact with the suffering of the world, and the "Eli, Eli" from the cross. Such transformation can only take place, however, if there is an initial and ongoing meeting on the ground of the person's own experience.

USING RITUAL WITH INDIVIDUALS

One pastor, when asked what was special about *pastoral* counseling, told me, "You can bless people." The answer took me aback; no one else I'd asked had suggested such a thing. Here was one more sign of the split that has grown up between ritual and the counseling function. Yet the fact remains, I thought, that even if a pastor wouldn't dream of doing any ritual in the counseling room, the person coming to her generally knows her as one who blesses and declares forgiveness and serves a holy meal. The associations people have in connection with a minister are ritual ones, as well as moral and religious ones. They may expect her to cast moral judgments, or to live as an example to others, or to be more "spiritual" than other folks. They may see her as an authority figure exercising benign or restrictive parental influence. They may see her as one who has volunteered her life in the service of humanity, and thus as a resource for free counseling and other social services. Any of these expectations would have an effect on the counseling relationship. But the one association everyone has to pastors is one seldom mentioned in counseling circles: they lead worship. Alongside the various social roles and stereotypes and the parental projections stands the pastor's ritual role and authority. At times when people need a sense of order or meaning, a handle on ambivalence or an approach to mystery, it may be the ritual authority of the pastor that draws them, even if they do not consciously define their need as having any ritual dimension.

This does not mean that pastors should include ritual actions in all their counseling relationships. It does mean that the minister's function as ritualizer colors all pastoral relationships, by holding out the possibility of access to a symbolic world large enough and powerful enough to embrace the most intractable events of life and death. Everyone asks, at some level or another, for symbols adequate to their own need, joy, and pain, to the need, joy, and pain of the world around them. The pastor needs to be aware of the symbolic dimensions of this search, and to feel at home with the words and images and actions that will carry the tradition's symbolic power. Sometimes the best way to convey these symbols is through informal conversation or simple attentive presence. Often, however, there are opportunities for spontaneous or semiformalized ritual expressions of the church's world view. When conversation stumbles, there may be a prayer or a ritual touch, to heal or bless or absolve. When all else fails, there may be a wordless kneeling together, a symbol of the community of beseeching that goes deeper than the isolating silence.

Prayer

The ritual most commonly requested of pastors is prayer. Whether a prayer is improvised or read from a book, it is a ritual. Even casual prayers are conventionalized in their form of address to God, their syntax, their norms guiding what can and can't be said, and the bodily attitude that accompanies them. The conventions governing these elements of prayer vary widely among American Christian groups. There are those who hold hands and those who fold them; there are those who identify sincerity with work-a-day syntax ("O God, I just want to say how good it is to be here") and those who cling to the Edwardian English of the old Book of Common Prayer. Since a minister can no longer assume that his congregation shares a cohesive ethnic tradition of piety and forms of prayer, his first task is to find out how this particular person feels at home in prayer.

In introducing this chapter, I pointed out that a pastor may use prayer to fend off a person's needs. In such cases the ritual words are used to model the "correct" attitude, and to rule out any "impious" questions, "faithless" protests, or other "wrong" thoughts. This happens far more often than any of us would like to admit. The pastor prays by the patient's bedside: "O God, we know that everything that happens to us is in accordance with your loving will. We believe that everything works to the good for those who love you, and we trust your plan for our lives. Help John to accept this illness willingly at your hands and to bear his cross cheerfully." At worst, the prayer may even include a more explicit condemnation of "bad" thoughts or feelings: "We repent of the weakness of faith which leads us to question your purposes, and the impatience which tempts us to rebel against your will." Such prayers are a ritual use of a distorted doctrine of the divine will for the purpose of suppressing "incorrect" feelings. This will-of-God talk is just one example of ritual suppression; other distorted doctrines may serve equally well to define away or condemn a person's state of mind. Anger or even sadness may be defined as sin and "confessed" or denied expression. A need for conflict resolution may be ignored while the pastor pleads on the person's behalf for humility and patience.

It is not only in ritual that such things are said, of course. Any of these assaults by a misbegotten piety on human feeling and need may be carried out in pastoral conversation as well as in prayer. The difference in *praying* them is significant, however. First, the setting and syntax of prayer may give the ideas added ritual authority. Second, the convention of prayer does not generally allow the parishioner to question what the pastor says until the prayer is over (if then). All the more reason for the pastor to listen before she prays!

When prayer grows out of listening, it can be a way into the need, rather than a way around it. Having listened to a patient's anger and confusion, one chaplain began to pray this way: "O God, you know how hard it is for us to come to you at a time like this. You know how we feel torn between wanting to trust you and feeling angry about what's happened. . . ." Expressing the anger nonjudgmentally this way in the context of prayer acts as a kind of validation, an indication that the statement of such a feeling can be accepted not only by the chaplain but by God. Several chaplains have told me that this sort of empathic prayer can move the conversation to a deeper level. Just as the admonitory prayer can cut off the expression of spiritual and emotional need, so a prayer born of listening can encourage such expression. By putting some of the patient's feelings into the prayer, the chaplain has said that *all* the patient's experience is worthy of God's own attention. When my experience is taken that seriously, I am more likely to share more of it.

Blessing

Blessing is another simple ritual, often neglected by Protestants. One eight-year-old child confided in me that she envied her Catholic friends because they could get blessings for themselves and even their pets. She wished her pastor would bless her, but she was embarrassed to ask because she figured Protestants didn't do that. She had felt guilty when she "baptized" her own cat, thinking it probably wasn't right. Now, one would have to get to know this child well to begin guessing at the psychological and spiritual meanings this wish had for her. It does demonstrate, though, that there may be unvoiced ritual needs in quite unexpected places. Interestingly, an educator who has asked many people their childhood memories of worship told me that they often speak about the benediction. They usually insist that they looked forward to it not (at least, not only) because it heralded the end of a long service, but for its own sake, out of fascination with the word and gesture. These were adults who had not communed as children so, in part, the benediction may have been the part of the service that touched them most directly.

Unfortunately, blessing is not something that comes naturally to many pastors. As I pointed out in the introduction, Paul Pruyser suggests that pastoral benedictions have deteriorated due to the decline of belief in providence.[1] Pruyser thinks that ministers can't bless with power and conviction because they aren't theologically certain that God has any direct effect on the events of our lives. I would wager that any such theoretical implications are one step removed from the salient issue: that of ritual role-expectations. If pastors are poor at blessing it is often because they are ill at ease with ritual authority. They view the power of blessing as hierarchical or even magical in a negative sense. It seems to conflict with their sense of democracy and their egalitarian models of the church and the pastoral role.

It is true that there is a functional hierarchy in the act of blessing, as in all ritual, and all ordered human interaction, for that matter. Ritual authority in a Christian context, however, is invested primarily in the words and actions because they derive from the invitation of God, and only derivatively in the person of the ritualizer, as a means to the end of extending God's invitation reliably. What needs to be renewed is the confidence in God's intention to come to us through human symbols of word and gesture. When God's invitation is understood as the basis of ritual authority, it is possible to avoid both the arrogance of ministers who like to be above the crowd and the wishy-washy delivery of those who are authority-shy. A lively sense of grace will put the authority where it belongs and produce some surprises.

One such surprise befell a pastor I know in a ritual of blessing. One Easter, a woman in his parish wanted the work she was beginning blessed. In part to avoid negative associations with church hierarchy from the woman's past, they decided to make it a mutual blessing. They wrote a general blessing of vocation beforehand, and each one said these words with personalized additions, while laying hands on the other's head. The pastor's surprise was that he found himself deeply moved by the woman's benediction and felt blessed beyond any expectation. He had agreed to it primarily because of what it would mean to her and found a ritual need met that he had not known was there. The power of the ritual worked like a river carving its own channel and in the process showed that "hierarchical" ritual authority can be exercised with the deepest mutuality.

Blessings can happen in less formal ways, without kneeling or the laying on of hands, and still be an authoritative communication of God's affirming presence. One such blessing took place in the pastoral counseling of a minister in vocational crisis. This minister was the son of a minister, and the father was critical of both the son and his vocation. The son kept hoping for his father's approval, only to meet renewed rejection. Other factors in the son's life had now brought him to a crisis of self-doubt, as he questioned his vocation and his worth. His counselor, himself a pastor, at one point told him: "I'm glad you're a pastor; what you are is a gift to the church." This simple statement was a transforming moment for the client.

He had been on his way out of parish ministry, and this word of approbation was the beginning of a dramatic reversal which led him into a renewed commitment to his vocation. True, this was probably in part a "transference cure"—the pastoral counselor was invested by transference with paternal authority so that he could give the fatherly blessing the client had always sought in vain. But all human authority derives in part from the force of parental transference. The counselor's blessing drew not only on father-transference, but on the authority of the church (symbolized by the counselor's ordination) and ultimately the authority of God. Coming from a pastor, this informal "blessing" implied that the client was God's gift to the church, that his vocation was valued by God.

The need for a blessing can be especially strong at a time of transition for which no formal ritual has been developed. Starting a new job or retiring may be times for blessings focusing on the vocation of baptism. Moving can be a major disruption in people's lives, and a house blessing can be a positive note in the transition. The children's picturebook *Mrs. Moskowitz and the Sabbath Candles*[2] tells of a widow's move from her longtime home to an apartment and her reluctance to settle in. Finally, the impetus to unpack the boxes and clean and decorate comes from the need to celebrate the approaching Sabbath. I have found that house blessings work in a similar way for me; I am willing to have guests visit when boxes are still lying around, but several months after my last move, I was finally motivated to unpack those last boxes only by the prospect of the house blessing. In a culture of great mobility and constant transitions, we might investigate the possibility of blessings that will root us where we are for now and affirm God's presence from here on out.

Confession and Absolution

Do people have a sense of sin anymore? In the face of cultural pluralism, the church's moral catechesis, though it may have gained maturity and sensitivity, has certainly deteriorated in authority and clarity. Yet the sense of sin, though confused and submerged, does not seem to be extinct in people today. It seems to surface especially at times of crisis, such as illness, the breakdown of a relationship, or midlife self-assessment. One hospital chaplain, a Roman Catholic laywoman, told me, "I hear confessions all the time. They want to know if this is happening to them because they cheated on their wife, or because they were mean to their mother." A nurse told me of being with a dying man who was slipping in and out of consciousness, and who was terribly distressed over something he felt he had done wrong; she had to tell him over and over that God still loved him and would forgive him. Perhaps people today are not different; perhaps it has always been true that most people will not take a hard look at themselves as long as things are going along fairly smoothly. Crisis and confession may be natural companions.

A distinction must be made, however, between the sense of sin and the presence of sin, between guilt feelings and guilt. The confusion can go both ways in our culture. People may go to a therapist to handle their "guilt feelings" when their guilt is real, and what they need to do is apologize or make reparation. The New York public TV station years ago ran a spot showing a person in analysis, whose analyst told him he wasn't neurotically guilty at all; he was *really* guilty, because he watched Channel 13 and didn't subscribe. A real-life example of this sort of confusion came after the space shuttle blew up. The Morton Thiokol engineers, who had all felt the shuttle should not be launched but had had their recommendation overridden by management, stopped short of trying to circumvent their bosses and contact NASA directly. After the explosion, they felt guilty, and the company engaged a psychiatrist to help them work through this. Was their guilt a psychiatric problem?

The minister will have to deal with the confusion in the other direction, when people confess to sin out of a false sense of guilt. The minister must work at distinguishing between neurotic feelings of badness and realistic shame and regret. Does the person feel guilty about how she treated her father because she really did neglect him culpably, or because the father had convinced her years ago that she owed him total, lifelong devotion? Does she feel she failed in her duties as a wife because her husband abandoned her? Is she suffering from the mixture of appropriate regret and unrealistic guilt we all feel when a loved one dies? Is she making a case for her own guilt in order to find an explanation for an illness or accident that has befallen her? That is, does she need to justify what has happened to her as punishment in order for the world to make sense, or for God to be good? Does her guilt arise from having feelings that she's been taught to see as un-Christian (anger, resentment of other's demands, or even grief)?

If the guilt does seem neurotic or inappropriate, a delicate pastoral problem arises. One wouldn't want to seem to verify a person's neurotic sense of guilt by telling him he was forgiven. Besides, absolutions rarely have much impact (psychologically speaking) on neurotic guilt; he won't "feel forgiven." The medieval confessors were aware of such problems and wrote about how to deal with the "scrupulosity" of depressed or obsessive-compulsive penitents. The confessors turned to consoling the penitent, or admonishing him for his lack of trust in divine grace. Unfortunately, admonishment only compounds the problem, and even consolation is tricky. An assurance of God's unconditional love is always appropriate, but the pastor must be careful not to seem to dismiss the person's concern. One woman confessed her techniques of procrastination only to have the priest tell her, "Come back when you have some real sins to confess." If he was trying to kid her into a sense of perspective he failed miserably; his remark served only to make her feel devalued and patronized. Guilt feelings, however neurotic, must be listened to attentively and explored. Then, if necessary, the assurance of God's love may be accompanied by a referral to therapy.

There are all sorts of ritual variations possible in confession and absolution, formal and casual, old and new.[3] Sometimes a conversation about grace is most appropriate. Sometimes a definite symbolic gesture or word is more reassuring and effective than talk alone. The pastor might suggest saying the formula for absolution used on Sundays, or she might improvise the words but ritually underscore them with a gesture, such as the laying on of hands or the greeting of peace. She might use gestures that recall the connection between forgiveness and baptism—for example, making the sign of the cross on the person's forehead. One pastor takes people from his office to the font when the time comes for the absolution and pours the water over their hands or uses it to mark a cross. Another keeps a baptismal candle in his study and lights it when the talk turns to the meaning of baptism and the promise of forgiveness. The rites set down in books, even the new ones, may feel awkward to those unaccustomed to such ritual, too formal or constrained, but one should not on that account give up on ritual expressions of forgiveness. One woman, a former Roman Catholic, was pleasantly surprised when she went to a woman pastor for private confession. Not only had the pastor typed up a possible form for them to use (they had talked about the overly hierarchical and noninclusive character of the traditional rite); she had also set a small table for them to sit at, furnished with several appropriate symbols. There is a parable there: coming to confess and finding the table set for you. The newest and most personalized ritual acts can speak the powerful language of the church's symbolic tradition.

Rites of Healing

When the liturgical movement brought to everyone's awareness the original intent of "extreme unction" as a rite of healing (rather than a "last-minute" rite), there was a readiness in the liturgical churches to develop true rites of healing. The old suspicions about hucksterism and superstition were partially offset by a new appreciation in the church and the society at large of the interaction of body, mind, and spirit. This understanding was highlighted by the wholistic health movement, which drew attention to the healing ministry of Jesus and to the connection between health and salvation. Now the Roman Catholic, Episcopal, and Lutheran churches all provide forms for both individual and corporate rites of healing. There are now a number of excellent resources on the pastoral practice of rites of healing.[4]

One of the recurrent themes in discussions of rites of healing is the psychological and spiritual importance of touch. The stories of Jesus' healing usually include a touch, and the Epistle of James recommends anointing along with prayer for the sick. Studies from psychology, ethology, and even physiology have reinforced our awareness of the fundamental importance of touch. It is a need that is intensified when a person is isolated by sickness. The hospitalized or homebound person may be geographically separated from friends and family. Others' irrational fear of infection may keep them at a distance, as we see now in the cruel shunning of persons with AIDS. The impersonality of much high-tech medical care compounds the problem. When I had my wisdom teeth removed, the surgeon who walked in after they'd started the anesthetic was someone whom I'd never seen before and whose name no one bothered to tell me. As the anesthetic started to take effect, and this stranger began to operate on me, I got very frightened. Luckily, the assisting doctor took my hand and held on to it throughout the procedure, which felt like a lifeline and kept my terror at bay. When I thanked him at the follow-up visit for holding on, he told me that they had given me a drug which had countered my "allergic reaction" and I couldn't possibly remember anything during the procedure because of the anesthetic. So much for the importance of a human touch!

If a virtually counterintentional touch like this doctor's can do so much good, imagine what good might be done by an intentional touch. For that is what the laying on of hands is: not a "magic" touch, but a fully intentional one, one that is meant to say something clearly and in doing so to convey God's healing power. The wisdom of the liturgy is that we pray with our whole selves, not just our minds and tongues; when we lay on hands we show that we pray for the other's whole self, body and soul together. The tendency of much of our prayer toward disembodied spirituality needs to be countered, especially when we are faced with the great physical need and social isolation of illness. The scent and feel of anointing with oil are a physical sign that recalls baptism for those who use oil in the baptismal rite. The Swedish Lutheran rite of anointing of the sick makes this baptismal connection explicit; this puts the focus on the symbolic meaning of the action of anointing and helps decrease the likelihood that the focus will be on the "magic" power of the oil itself. Where oil is not used in baptism, touching the sick person in the sign of the cross may serve the purpose of recalling baptism. The touch itself should last nearer a minute than a few seconds. Part of that time can be spent in silence; in fact, that's a helpful way to start in order to focus in. The accompanying prayer can use formal or informal language, as long as the words are chosen with care and spoken with attention to the moment. The touch will make it a very different sort of prayer from the prayer which the pastor directs to God, talking *about* the sick person while both bow their heads, not touching or looking at each other.

The use of such individual rites of healing may be particularly important in long-term illness, when the person's life is shaped by the disease and the pain or disability which it brings and perhaps the prospect of death as its outcome. The focus of prayer in such cases is likely to be less on recovery or cure and more on committing oneself to God's care. The concern may appropriately be the nature of the individual's baptismal vocation in the world as a person with a serious illness. The echoes of baptism in touch or word or oil may be especially important, because they provide a paschal framework for the experience of suffering and death. Through baptism our suffering, like all our life experience, is "hid with Christ in God." Though this is neither cure nor answer (the resurrection does not erase the cross), it is at least a connection with the life of God hidden in our wounded lives.

One thing always to remember in ministry to the sick is their general lack of control over their lives. The pastor visiting a sick person should try to give him as much autonomy as possible in the interaction between them. She should let him set the tone and duration of the conversation. If she offers to share a prayer or other ritual expression, she should explore its meaning with him and let him decide on what they will do. Especially when hospitalized, sick people have little say over what is done to them; religious ritual should not become another thing imposed upon them "for their own good." The general rule of pastoral ritual practice—that one begins by exploring the possibilities for ritual expression together and finding out what is meaningful to the parishioner—should be applied even more strictly when visiting the sick. In Jerome Berryman's essay in *The Sacred Play of Children,* he gives a good example of this approach in offering a rite of healing to a sick child. I am impressed with the way the child is introduced to the ritual, asked whether there is some part of his body he is especially concerned about and would like blessed, and generally given a say in designing the ritual experience.[5]

This is not to rule out the use of a rite of healing with someone who cannot express his or her wishes. Often someone who is unable to communicate may be especially in need of the connective power of ritual. One pastor described to me such an encounter with a person who had just had a stroke and was unable to speak. He was very agitated, seeming anxious and upset. As the pastor went through the rite of healing with him, anointing him and praying for him, he calmed down. The ritual brought a relaxing of tension and an apparent sense of peace. In part this may have been because the ritual established a connection which was not dependent on the patient's talking. Communication took place through touch and the pastor's words, and the sick man could participate in this communication by receiving the touch and responding physically through self-calming. The rite must have partially overcome the terrifying isolation that came with his inability to speak.

Another ritual which can do much to heal the isolation of the sick is communion. The celebration of the eucharist with someone confined to home or hospital can be a powerful sign of the bond of community within the body of Christ which overcomes our isolation. To do this, the ritual should be as communal as possible, including others present besides the patient, bringing other visitors from the church along with the pastor or lay minister of communion. If the worshiping community can only include pastor and patient, one should at least refer to the larger community in word and symbol, perhaps bringing the bread and wine from the community's celebration. One seminarian doing CPE visited a woman in the university hospital who had just delivered her baby far from family and friends, and who was feeling very lonely and isolated. She was deeply grateful when he celebrated the eucharist with her on Sunday morning because, she said, she felt it united her with her faraway relatives and friends, who she knew were also communing that morning. They were eating at the same table at the same time, so distance could not really separate them.

Ritual with the Dying

As the Roman Catholics have restored extreme unction to its original intention as a rite of healing, and as other churches are discovering the rich possibilities of pastoral liturgy, new rites for the time of dying have been created. This task is complicated by the changes in our way of dying. It is less common now for a person to be conscious just before death, as medical techniques sustain partial life for longer periods. If people die outside the hospital, it is usually a sudden and unexpected death. If they die in the hospital, they are often "out of it" before the end comes. Too often, due to the doctors' never-say-die training or their understandable fear of lawsuits, those with an insignificant chance at life are resuscitated and die surrounded by a painful chaos of machinery and intrusive strangers rather than by a vigil of family or friends. For all these reasons, there will be many times when no ritual with the dying person as participant is possible immediately before death.

Yet there may be significant possibilities for ritual care near the time of death. If the dying person is unconscious, the commendation may be prayed for the sake of family and friends gathered around, as a way of their saying good-bye. Besides, people have been known to remember things said while they were unconscious; thus the dying person may be more "present" in the ritual than you think. If the person is conscious, various sorts of prayer and ritual may provide one dimension of a deeply personal communication among those gathered. The type of ritual expression appropriate would vary widely according to the personality and religious style of the dying person, and the circumstances of the death. A number of people writing about the process of dying have observed that often the patient comes to terms with the fact that she is dying before the family does. Sometimes, she then finds it difficult to "let go" because she senses that her family is not ready to let her go. In such cases, the use of a rite of commendation with the family may be a way of their giving her permission to die.

One young woman lost a friend of about her own age to a lingering death from cancer. (I will call her Kay, and the dying friend Lisa.) It happened that Kay was "on duty" when death came. Early in the shift she sensed that Lisa was failing and offered to read the prayer for the dying in the Lutheran prayer book. She softened the suggestion by saying, "We'll probably laugh about this tomorrow, but is it OK if I read this?" Lisa indicated agreement and appeared to respond to the prayer with gratitude. Kay later said it seemed to express all the feelings they'd gone through together in the last weeks. Later in the evening, Lisa was drifting in and out of contact, and at times would appear to get frightened. Then Kay spoke to her in a more personalized and simpler rite of reassurance, as one might speak to a small child. She listed all the people close to Lisa in a litany of love, saying, "I love you, Susan loves you, John loves you, your mother loves you . . ." and always ending with "Jesus loves you, and God loves you." This would calm Lisa's fears, and Kay repeated it over and over, until the end came peacefully. Both rituals were appropriate at their time, the formal prayer and the simple litany of reassurance, and both helped meet Kay's needs as well as Lisa's. The ritual statements infused with peace and deep meaning a time that might otherwise have been anxious and empty. The prayer helped Kay communicate her awareness that death was near, while the litany helped Lisa overcome her fears (which in the last days had at times overwhelmed her). In both these ways, ritual brought Kay and Lisa together when Lisa might otherwise have felt totally isolated, in her awareness of dying and her fear of abandonment.

As communion can be important to the sick in overcoming their sense of isolation, so can it also be important for the dying. Another meaning of the eucharist is also particularly significant in the face of death: its eschatological character, as a "foretaste of the feast to come." This dimension of the eucharist became the focus of a wish for communion in one small girl dying of a brain tumor. This six-year-old child, who had been sick for two years, had listened to her pastor talk about the eucharist in resurrection language, as a victory banquet. She asked for communion because, she said, she wanted to be at God's party. Though her denomination generally did not commune children as young as she, the pastor made an exception in her case, and began to discuss with her the meaning of the eucharist. Preparation for participation in the sacrament was for her a preparation for death, and for resurrection—God's party. She showed an absolute faith and the fearlessness that Elisabeth Kübler-Ross has so often found in dying children. She received her first and last communion two days before she lost consciousness. The sacrament gave her a way to share with her pastor and her family her understanding of dying, and it gave them all a way to experience Christ's presence in the face of death.

The accent in these last stories has been on the ritual as a bearer of positive feelings and meanings, a firm reassurance and ground of hope. It is important to note that at the time of dying, as at any other time, ritual should be large enough to embrace all our ambivalence. When we face death in another's dying, we may want only to reassure for our own sake, to comfort ourselves. That may not be the best comfort for the one who is dying; that person may feel connected in the face of separation only by having his pain and protest held up to God in prayer. One pastor was visiting a man who had just decided to go off dialysis treatment. She was about to read Psalm 23, when he stopped her: "Pastor, no; when I wake up at night, what I read is Psalm 22." Luckily he knew what he needed and could ask for it, and had a pastor who would respond by letting him share his experience of forsakenness. Many people cannot ask so clearly. The pastor needs to provide a range of images, biblical stories, and other rich symbols in prayer, conversation, and ritual, so that each person can find what speaks to him. Some Christians will die with serene foresight into the future and forgiveness for all, like Jesus in Luke's Gospel; others will die with an agonized question, like Jesus in the Gospel of Mark. The symbolic riches of the tradition are there, able to hold all our humanness; the pastor needs to listen well and then to use those symbols to bear our need and God's presence.

Ritual with the Grieving

When a death is foreseen, the ritual care of the dying person's circle of friends and/or family can start before death. One of the ways to use ritual as the focus for beginning the grieving process is to plan the funeral ahead of time. Many families have found it a deeply moving experience to plan the funeral or memorial service together. It can be a time for family members and friends to say some of the things to the dying person that otherwise might not be said until the wake or funeral: what they value most about her, what their favorite memories are, why they would want to sing a certain song. The pastor can take this opportunity to make sure that children also get a chance to tell how they feel about saying good-bye, and, if they choose, to contribute to the service. If all involved are up to such a discussion, it can provide a framework for the expression of feelings that otherwise might not be voiced. The planning process can also help create a sense of ownership of the funeral rite itself, which will likely make it more meaningful to all concerned.

Rites of farewell to be celebrated at the time of death have already been discussed. Perhaps one further note is appropriate here, though, when thinking of the family's needs. It is significant that the new Lutheran book of *Occasional Services* includes in its rite of commendation a prayer for use when a life-support system is withdrawn. I am told that this prayer was a compromise; numerous chaplains had requested a separate rite for such an occasion, but the ethical issues involved had not yet been settled by the Lutheran church bodies. Even though there is just this single, rather vague, compromise of a prayer, it still played a powerful role for one man whose wife was brain-dead. The woman had been hurt in an automobile accident when her husband was driving, and though it had not been his fault, he still felt responsible. He didn't want to authorize the doctors to turn off the life-support system for two reasons. First, it would mean that he really had killed her; and second, it would mean that she was irrevocably gone and he would be all alone. His pastor let him express his feelings of guilt and anxiety over the decision, and discussed with him the various ethical and theological considerations. He kept trying to assure the grieving husband that God is not legalistic, not "hung up on a heartbeat," but relates to us in grace, and that the real life-or-death decision was finally God's and not his responsibility. When the husband came to the decision to authorize the withdrawal of life support, the pastor came to stay with him at the bedside when the machines were shut off, and they prayed together the rite of commendation, including the special prayer. The discussion and the rite, taken together, recast the meaning of the event in the husband's mind. He did not afterward feel at all as though he had killed his wife; rather, he felt that he was trusting God to do what God wanted to do with her. The pastor felt the rite with its prayer to mark the cessation of life support did at least three important things. First, it simply provided something else to focus on alongside the apparently purely "negative" action of shutting off the machine. Second, the specific prayer, simply by being there in the official book, did supply a kind of church sanction to the decision to withdraw life support. Third, participating in the ritual with the pastor gave the husband a sense that he was not alone after all. As he told the pastor later: "The miracle was that God was there when she died."

Starting immediately after the death, there may be various occasions when the family would accept the minister's offer of a ritual of grieving in the home. These occasions may include, for example, a pre-funeral vigil, or a litany of family prayer in the weeks after the funeral, or the recognition of some subsequent anniversary. One pastor described to me how he adapts such occasional rites to the family's religious style and emotional needs. For example, he told me that many Scandinavians have been socialized never to express strong emotion. When he prays with such a family after a death, he takes the rite at a very slow, gentle pace, leaving long stretches of silence to facilitate the expression of grief. He also weaves in biblical stories that are appropriate to the occasion; when a child has died, for instance, he might express the hope of the resurrection in prayer through a reference to Jairus's daughter.

For the circle of friends and family closest to the person who dies, the funeral is not likely to be able to help them "work through" or resolve their grief, unless the death was long-expected and most of the grief has been worked through before death occurs. For many people, the most the funeral can do is to get them out of the initial state of shock, numbness, and denial, and *into* grief, that is, to help them into rather than through or out of grief. This is why the crucial moments for the family and close friends are usually the signs of finality: the closing of the casket, the lowering of the casket into the ground, the first shovelful of dirt. It is often helpful for the pastor to be with the family when the casket is closed, to pray or just to arrange the focused quietness the family needs to take in this moment. Unfortunately it rarely happens now in the United States that the casket is lowered into the ground while the people are still there. One reason this is avoided by the professionals involved is precisely that it can be a moment of high emotion, of facing finality, and perhaps crying out in protest. Some rabbis and pastors insist on the casket's being lowered while the mourners are still there to watch, out of the conviction that this is an important ritual moment of truth. The mourners will seesaw between denial and acceptance for a long time to come, but ritual honesty and care for healthy grieving both require that the funeral state clearly that the one they mourn is gone from this world forever.

If the funeral marks the onset of mourning, what rituals are there to mark its progress over the next year and after? Unfortunately the Christian tradition is poor in such rites; the Jewish tradition is far richer in pastoral ritual in this area. There are some prayers written for the anniversary of a death. Mention of at least the first anniversary of a death can be made in the prayer of the church on Sunday. It should be remembered that the ritual occasions of the first year following a death are particularly important milestones in grieving: the first Christmas without Dad, the first Easter, the first wedding anniversary. A family might find it healthier to visit the grave together at the beginning of the Christmas holiday to say good-bye again, rather than to attempt to celebrate the holiday tiptoeing around the subject of their loss.

Many parishes have the tradition of including in the prayer on All Saints' Sunday the names of all those in the parish who have died in the past year. A pastor in one community that did this told me that it was especially helpful for those whose loved ones had died at least several months previously; for the others, it came too close to the death to help mark a shift out of acute grief. Similarly, John Westerhoff tells of his time in a parish in New England, where burials could not take place in the frozen ground of winter. When someone died in winter the funeral was held immediately but the burial occurred after the spring thaw. Westerhoff observed that, in the case of a tragic, unexpected death, the families who experienced this winter funeral/spring burial pattern seemed to show a better adjustment in their grieving than those for whom funeral and burial came together.[6] When events do not supply such a natural opportunity, we need to search with individual families for appropriate ways to mark later waystations along the path of bereavement.

IDENTIFYING RITUAL NEEDS

Even when the person coming to a pastor does not ask for ritual or prayer, and even when there is no specific situation such as illness that fits an existing ritual, the pastor can still be alert to ritual possibilities in counseling and other pastoral situations. Does the person have needs which might be met in part by ritual care? Is there a need for confirmation of identity, for affirmation by the community, for recognition of a significant passage? For healing or blessing? Is there a need to symbolize gratitude, to mark some special time, to say good-bye or to remember the dead? In any of these situations and many others, the pastor might suggest some kind of symbolic action or ritual observance in addition to pastoral conversation. Pastor and parishioner can discuss various ritual possibilities, until they settle on one that feels right to both of them, not silly or overly formal. It might free up the beginning of this process to start with fantasy: what would you do to mark this occasion if you could do anything you wanted, have anyone you wanted to participate come? The answer to such a question would be enlightening for its own sake!

The ritual appropriate to the situation will not always be one performed by the pastor. Sometimes a person's need will be to design a ritual or symbolic expression herself, and she may want the pastor there as participant, witness, or silent legitimator. She may want the pastor to come with her to the cemetery as she faces her father's grave and says what she needs to say; she may not want him to say or do anything but be there and "bless" the event with his symbolic presence. This opportunity to design one's own ritual response to an event may be particularly helpful for a child, for whom the adult ritual may be inappropriate, inaccessible, or ill-timed.[7] Designing her own ritual, and perhaps having an adult (pastor, parent, teacher) participate in it, may help her regain a sense of control in the face of a threatening change or overwhelming tragedy.

One need which pervades our lives is the need for an assurance of God's love and our identity as children of that love. It is a strong Reformation tradition of pastoral care to direct people to the sacraments as witnesses and guarantors of God's gracious love for them. Luther spoke of the promise we hear in God's word as being like a will which makes us heirs, and said that the sacraments are the official seal on that will. It is the seal which allows us to trust that the document means what it says: that it indeed comes from the one with power to give, and that the giver truly intended it for us. Or rather, intended it *for me*: for part of the importance of the sacramental seal is that it comes to us one by one, the promise intended for all humanity, but sealed "for me, for you." Another quality of the sacraments which gives them special power to assure and console is their objectivity. Luther always maintained that only faith could receive the promise in the sacraments, but that faith rested in the objective, external, tangible sign of grace. At times when our subjective world is all confusion, the tangible promise can provide a touchstone for faith.

When the appeal is to the objective witness of the sacraments, it makes sense to enrich the pastoral conversation with the use of tangible symbols which recall or convey the sacramental promise. This may mean bringing communion to those who cannot come to church. It may mean standing by the font and playing with the water as you talk, or anointing with oil to renew the Spirit's gifts of baptismal vocation and healing power. One woman found it difficult to take comfort in her baptism because she envisioned her mother holding her at the font, and her deep fear of her mother made that a terrifying scene colored by fantasies of drowning. After much conversation, this woman and her pastor decided that her ritual need was for a symbolic reinterpretation of her baptism that would free it from its association with her mother's destructive control. With this in mind, at the end of the next Easter Vigil (a service new to the woman, and thus free of maternal associations) the pastor lit a baptismal candle for her from the new paschal candle. She later told him that seeing her candle lit from the paschal gave her a new, alternative image of her baptism, one which linked it directly to the dying and rising of Christ. The promise of Easter had come to her as she stood far beyond the reach of her mother's arms, and she could safely claim it as her own. Lighting the baptismal candle became an important symbol for her, a focus for her prayer—especially when she needed reassurance that her baptism was a gift of life that was *not* in her mother's hands. The candle could not have meant this to her apart from all their conversations, but the conversations would have taken longer to transform her praying if she had not been able to see the promise shining before her eyes.

In the sections which follow, more specific areas of ritual need will be pursued. Stillbirth will be discussed as an occasion that brings with it ritual needs which are often unmet or poorly understood; this discussion will serve as a case study of identifying ritual needs. Then I will bring up some special considerations in doing ritual with people who are cognitively impaired and with those who have psychiatric problems.

The Case of Stillbirth

The event of stillbirth is a helpful one to study in terms of ritual need. The needs of parents who have lost a hoped-for child before or at birth are just beginning to be given serious attention, and among those needs are some which might be met by ritual. Cases of late miscarriage, stillbirth, or neonatal death provide examples of ritual confusion, and of some common mistakes made in approaching issues of ritual care.

The most prevalent ritual dilemma arises when the mother or other relative requests that the miscarried fetus or stillborn infant be baptized. Let me first discuss what is often done in such situations and why; then I will turn to an examination of the ritual needs behind the request. I have heard from a dozen seminarians from different schools, who were in CPE programs in hospitals across the country, that they were expected as part of their duties to perform a baptism whenever the parents requested it. I have no evidence as to how widespread this policy is in chaplaincy departments; I am concerned here only with what was behind the policy in these cases. What was interesting in each of these instances was the response to the seminarians' attempts to question this policy. They were made to feel that they were being rigid about the theological theory rather than being empathic to the parents' needs. One was told by her supervisor that the mother was in acute grief and this was no time for a lecture on the theology of baptism—"as if," said the seminarian, "I would have gone in and harangued the woman on her incorrect theology." What seems to be active behind these responses to the seminarians is the old split between counselors and ritualists, surfacing through the conflict between the therapeutic norm and the theological norm for ritual action. The assumption was that, if the parents asked for a baptism and thought that it would make them feel better or help them cope with the crisis, then there could be no reason not to perform it. Another supervisor put it this way: "The baby's dead, so it doesn't matter what you do to it; it's the parents' needs you should be ministering to. Why not do it if it makes them feel better?"

There are two problematic assumptions in these supervisors' line of reasoning. One is the assumption that the only relevant norm is the therapeutic norm, which seems to be defined in terms of the measurable, immediate effect on the feelings of the living. The introduction of other normative dimensions into the discussion was judged unempathic by these chaplains prima facie, even when it was done in CPE-group discussions and not on the scene. The normative issues of ritual honesty and the meaning of baptism are overridden by pastoral considerations. The understanding of what is "pastoral" here, however, brings into focus the second questionable assumption: that performing the baptism as requested is the best way to meet these parents' ritual needs. These particular chaplains were so caught up in contrasting rigidity about ritual meanings with pastoral empathy that it never occurred to them that there might be a *better* ritual response to the parents' need: one which would be more emphathic precisely because it was more appropriate to their tragic situation. In other words, it never occurred to these chaplains that ritual honesty is itself a pastoral concern.

What are some of the ritual needs commonly felt by people for whom parenthood and bereavement coincide? Three needs which might be met in part by ritual recur in people's stories of their experiences in the literature on stillbirth. First, the parents need others to recognize the reality of both the baby's existence and the parents' grief. It is all too common for people to respond to a late miscarriage or stillbirth by telling the parents in countless ways, "It never really existed, so you can't feel grief." Sometimes this is an effort to deny the awfulness of what has happened; sometimes it is just a completely wrongheaded attempt to comfort: "Well, at least you didn't have time to love him." There is no greater affront to a grieving person than telling her she has no reason to grieve, but this happens to these bereaved parents all the time. This message is just reinforced when the religious community offers no ritual response to their situation. One mother said that when the rabbi told her that there are no rituals for a stillborn child, she felt "like an illegitimate mourner."[8]

A second common ritual need is to commend the child to God. This is a dimension of the religious response whenever a loved one dies, but it is intensified when parents lose a small child. The parents wish so much to care for the child themselves, to protect it, and are deprived of that power by death, so the need to place the child into God's care is all the stronger. Third, there is a ritual need to say good-bye, to acknowledge an irrevocable loss and to begin to let go of all the hopes and dreams that were bound up in the anticipation of this infant's birth.

What sort of ritual might meet these needs? One ritual act which parents frequently express a wish for is the naming of the infant. This is a way of recognizing the individual existence of the child (and thus the reality of their loss), and of expressing their love and care for her. It is also a way of acknowledging the death of all the hopes and plans and expectations which grew during the pregnancy, by bestowing the name of the wished-for child on this dead infant. If parents were given the opportunity to do this, it might decrease the likelihood that they would give the "unused" name to their next same-sex child, a naming which too often carries with it a burden of unresolved grief.

In addition to naming, other appropriate ritual actions could include prayers which place the child in God's arms, perhaps a direct blessing of the infant, prayers and readings which acknowledge anger, grief, and questions, such as psalms of lament, as well as those which recall God's presence in our sorrow and promise for our future. As always in designing rituals, one should search the tradition for symbols which speak to the situation. One might, for example, refer to the death of Moses: all that long time of preparation and hope and struggle, and then death, death before the Jordan's (baptismal) waters, death just on the verge of the promised culmination—and yet a holy death nonetheless, a death hidden in God. Along with the traditional symbols there may be some very personal ones. A father may wish to sing a lullaby to his child, a sister may give him one of her toys. Some of these ritual acts may accompany a naming in the hospital, others may find their place in a funeral or memorial service.

The likelihood is that the majority of parents who request baptism for a stillborn or miscarried infant do so because baptism is the only ritual they know to ask for: because it is the rite for babies, and they want this one recognized as a baby; because it is the rite for naming, and they wish to name their child. If the chaplain or pastor offers a ritual which meets their special needs, it is unlikely that they would insist on a baptism. The chaplain Ronna Case, in her excellent article titled "When Birth Is Also a Funeral,"[9] advocates creating a rite for stillbirths which would combine elements of baptism (naming, prayer for God's care) with elements of the funeral (committal, symbols of grief). One friend of mine, when asked by a mother to baptize her dead infant, told her, "We have a special prayer for this situation," and he prayed over the infant's body a prayer of blessing and committal. The mother accepted this act of ritual care gratefully. She may have felt it as a *better* answer to her ritual need, because she knew her need was special, that this was *not* the same as having a living baby. The honesty, authority, and appropriateness of this ritual response all helped make it good pastoral care.

Ritual with People Who Are Mentally Impaired

Ritual is a cognitive as well as an affective experience; it can involve both our thinking and our feeling on many levels. People who have not developed or have lost certain cognitive capacities, such as long-term memory or abstract conceptual thought, will apprehend ritual somewhat differently. Such cognitive impairment can come with many conditions:

mental retardation, senility, brain disease or injury. Most people who are cognitively impaired can still participate in ritual and find it meaningful, and in fact many experience it more intensely through its affective and concrete-symbolic dimensions than do most cognitively "normal" people.

People who are called mentally retarded or developmentally disabled cover a broad range of I.Q.'s and an even broader range of personalities, needs, and talents. The most profoundly retarded individuals are likely to be institutionalized. Less severely retarded persons may be holding jobs, living on their own or with family or in group homes, getting married, and/or going to church. Nothing I say here will apply to all retarded persons, but there are some general comments that can be made about the ritual needs and gifts of many people who are moderately retarded. In general, then, people with less abstract conceptual skill will pick up more of the emotional and sensory aspects of ritual. Churches with a style of worship which is either emotive or sacramental (or both) will have more to offer to a mentally retarded individual than those whose worship is very "heady," all talk and abstract concepts and sitting still. The mentally retarded person, like the rest of us, will be more strongly engaged by what can be touched, tasted, and smelled than by words alone. These concrete symbols may include a flannelgraph story used in a children's sermon, but they may also include the richest traditional symbols of water, bread and wine, oil, light, and human touch. The fuller our liturgical symbols, the better they will be appropriated by the mentally retarded among us, and by the rest of us as well. Let the bread have taste, let the water be poured, let the bonfire be lit in the darkness of Easter Eve: we all need more sensuous liturgy.

Our use of liturgical symbols is very often impoverished by over-conceptualizing. First we focus on an abstract concept as if it expressed the full meaning of the symbol. Then we say that as long as we understand the concept it doesn't matter that the symbol itself is unprepossessing—if the bread tastes like paper or the washing doesn't get us wet. The focus of mentally retarded individuals on the concrete symbolic forms may help remind us of what we have lost. Sometimes indeed a retarded person can bring new meaning to a symbol by a concrete approach which has its own depth of insight. The *Lutheran* once carried a story about a Sunday School class in which everyone was given one of those plastic eggs that package nylons and told to put inside it a symbol of new life. Most of them put in flowers, butterflies, and such, except for the child with Down's Syndrome, who handed his egg in empty. When the eggs were opened, the children complained that somebody hadn't done it right, but this boy explained that he *had* done it—that his egg was empty, like the empty tomb.[10] Everyone else had produced conventional symbols with their normal cognition; his concrete thinking had found the symbol that all had missed, a symbol with more immediacy and power and connection with the Easter story than a thousand butterflies. Those who have learned at a different pace or from a different angle can contribute much to the community's vision.

There can be difficulties with some retarded persons in integrating them into the worship life of the community. Some profoundly retarded people may not be able to participate in the community worship, although such individuals are more likely to be living in institutions than at home. Even more moderately retarded children and adults may benefit from special services, at camps or churches with programs for the retarded, in addition to their attendance at regular worship services. Such special services can use a liturgy with simplified language, hymns with familiar or easily singable tunes and accompanying motions, audiovisual aids with homilies, etc.[11] Even given that such services can be great things, however, it is important that they not be used as an excuse to segregate retarded individuals from the community's worship against their own or their families' wishes. Parents are sometimes told, "Welcome, we're so glad you're here; you know, there are special services at the church down the street for children like your son." Such an attitude is a gross failure in hospitality.

The goal should always be to integrate the retarded person into the worshiping community. Retarded children and adults may not catch on to standards of appropriate behavior in formal situations as spontaneously as others, but most of them can learn these standards if clearly taught. Psychologists who work with the developmentally disabled educate them explicitly about how to behave at such events as concerts and plays (for instance, when to applaud). Parents, teachers, or pastors can ask such professionals for help in integrating retarded persons into the congregation's worship. As is true of everyone else in the congregation, retarded members should as far as possible be involved not only as quiet observers but as participants. Parents or teachers can teach them the liturgical responses and often-sung hymns; music is for many retarded persons a major joy of worship. They should be asked, like anyone in the congregation, to do anything else they're capable of, including ushering, bringing up the offering, and reading the lessons (in the regular version or in a simplified one such as the Basic English Bible).

More and more in the churches people are loosening up on the traditional cognitive prerequisites in the case of retarded children receiving communion. They are recognizing that faith is not defined predominantly by an intellectual grasp of abstract concepts and are finding new ways to catechize retarded children and adults. Once again, many of these methods are better education for everybody than the pure head-learning of old, for example, having the communion class all help bake the communion bread. Some churches have special curricula designed for sacramental preparation for retarded children. Where fewer resources exist, pastors and teachers may find materials in other ways; for instance, a Lutheran thirteen-year-old candidate for confirmation and first communion might be catechized with Roman Catholic first communion curricula aimed at seven-year-olds. First, though, a pastor with a retarded child in the congregation should check with denominational offices to see if materials and other helps are available, and if that fails, should try the offices of other theologically close denominations or the staff of church institutions that serve the mentally retarded. Happily, one hears fewer stories nowadays about retarded persons who have attended church faithfully all their lives and never been communed because they couldn't learn the catechism. The irony of the current more flexible approach to catechesis, of course, is that many churches end up communing retarded individuals with little cognitive grasp of the symbol's abstract meaning, while continuing to bar from the sacrament children who "understand" its meaning at least as well. I can only hope that our newfound insight into the faith of retarded persons will eventually help us see the faith of "normal" children as well.

Generally speaking, the rites of passage, such as adolescent confirmation, will be important to many retarded individuals, especially to those who are bothered by their problems in achieving some of society's marks of maturity, such as a driver's license. When retarded persons choose to marry, the church's blessing can be particularly important in the face of some people's uninformed and prejudiced objections to their marrying. Retarded persons need to mourn, of course, and if possible should be involved in the funeral and other rituals of mourning and farewell. If the person's cognitive limitations are severe enough that he doesn't understand the finality of death, this can be painful for all concerned; one young man was difficult to restrain at the funeral home because he kept trying to touch and call his sister to wake her up. That man was not brought to the funeral or gravesite committal, and one can sympathize with the family's decision. When possible, however, involvement should be encouraged and facilitated, perhaps by having a close family friend promise to stick by the retarded individual through the service. (That's often also a good idea with small children, when the parents or other family are too over-whelmed to pay close attention to them and answer difficult questions.) Years ago I attended the Quaker-style memorial service for a child, where anyone spoke who was so moved. It is the words of an older, retarded friend of the child that I remember most clearly; his immediate, present-tense, affectionate evocation of the little girl, though painful to listen to, helped us all to encounter our grief.

Mental retardation is only one kind of cognitive impairment. Persons who are senile or brain-injured have disturbances of thinking which are both similar to and quite different from the limitations of mentally retarded individuals. There is a wide range of cognitive disabilities to be considered here. What we identify as senility may be an actual case of degenerative Alzheimer's disease, or cognitive impairment of various kinds following strokes or other diseases affecting the brain, or a fogged state due to improper medication, or the cognitive fallout of an emotional problem such as depression or the disorientation following institutional-ization. Each of these has a different prognosis and a different set of prob-lems. In addition, there are the conditions resulting from disease or injury which affect the brain function of people at any age, in an astonishing variety of ways. I will concentrate here on the issue of deficits in memory, and their effect on ritual meaning.

The familiarity of ritual may offset even severe impairments of memory. I have heard again and again from pastors that ritual order will trigger a familiar, lifelong memory pattern even in senile people who are not track-ing at all well in the present. An Episcopal priest told me, "I can come in and the person can tell me the same story several times over, and yet as soon as I begin the eucharist she's *there*, following intently, giving the right responses." One Lutheran pastor goes to great lengths when visiting nurs-ing home residents to find out what rituals were familiar to them in their early years, in order that he might facilitate such ritual memory. He will perform services in the languages of their childhood, if they are immi-grants, or get others to record parts of such a service if it's a language he can't read. He will bring in ritual symbols they are familiar with: icons, votive candles, whatever. Once he even found the kind of incense that had been used in the Ukrainian Orthodox church of one man's background and burned it in the nursing home during their service. (Such a ministry, of course, is also appreciated by many older people who are fully "with it" mentally; they often like to hear the rites and hymns of their childhood, especially if they spoke something other than English in their early years.) As familiar rituals may trigger memory which allows a patterned response, so the uniform of a clergyperson can often cue a memory-impaired person to respond to the role even if she cannot recognize newly met individuals. She might not know who you are as an individual, but yet be able to recognize from your collar that you are a priest. "Oh, Father, thank you for coming," she can say, without having to grope for a name that won't come—another advantage of ritual roles.

In Oliver Sacks' book of essays on neurological case histories, *The Man Who Mistook His Wife for a Hat*, [12] there is the story of Jimmy, who has only very short-term memory for the present, and a long-term memory which his disease has erased back to 1945 or so, where he thinks he lives in an eternal present. Sacks speculated on the degree to which our "self" is a function of the continuity of life story provided by long-term memory and asked the nuns who ran the institution whether they thought Jimmy still had a soul. Indignantly, they told him to just watch Jimmy in chapel. Sacks reports that at mass Jimmy was indeed focused and present, able to concentrate with steady attention, caught up in a meaningful sequence of actions that had continuity over time—more than the few minutes that his short-term memory usually lasted. [13] So in other kinds of neurological damage as well, ritual can trigger memory and allow focused attention. This was not true of all Sacks' patients; some patients' symptoms blocked the ritual from their minds and caused them to act disruptively. Nonetheless, for many neurologically impaired persons, ritual memory can survive the dissolution of normal long-term memory and thus allow for meaningful ritual participation.

One older man whose wife developed Alzheimer's related to a conference on aging his terribly difficult times in taking care of her. Two stories stand out in my mind. One is that the congregation made him feel his wife was unwelcome because she (a former choir member) would forget herself and start singing along with the choir. The difficulties in teaching appropriate behavior are much greater with those who have brain disease or injury than with the mentally retarded. A person with Alzheimer's may understand your suggestion and then immediately forget it. One can understand the real problems and the frustration of the choir if she "ruined" their sound, but more caring certainly could have been communicated to the husband in this case, however the problem was handled.

The second story was that after the wife had become homebound, the pastor eventually stopped coming to give her communion, because she no longer "understood" what was happening. The historical position of the church on this issue is that if the person used to understand and believe when in sound mind, they should be given the benefit of the doubt. At the very least in this case, the home communions were a ministry to the husband, to whom they symbolized the church's continuing care for his wife. This restrictive use of cognitive criteria is legalism, not gospel-centered pastoral care. We need to explore ways, with the advice of professionals in the area of neurological disabilities, to expand our ritual sharing with those who are cognitively impaired.

Ritual with People Who Have Psychiatric Problems

There are even fewer generalizations to be made here than could be made in the last section on mental impairment. Psychiatric problems may range from the everyday conflicts of "normal neurotics" to the profound, in some cases biologically based, personality disturbance of psychoses. Most of the severely mentally ill people a pastor meets will be in treatment, and the pastor should check with the responsible therapist (with the patient's permission, of course, if that is at all possible) before offering any out-of-the-ordinary pastoral care. A less severely disturbed person, who can basically function on his own but has serious emotional problems, should be encouraged into therapy (with someone other than his parish pastor, please!). If he is in therapy, the pastor should encourage him to tell his therapist about the significant things they do together, so that the pastoral contact is not in competition with the therapy. If there is a request for some kind of ritual, or if the pastor thinks of suggesting a ritual action, another consideration should be kept in mind. The more emotionally conflicted or disturbed a person is, the more important it is to determine carefully the meaning ritual symbols hold for him before using them. The pastor should always ask: What religious symbols have you found especially meaningful, helpful, challenging? What images do you find disturbing or frightening? What are your best and worst memories of church ritual, from childhood, adolescence, adulthood? What are your favorite hymns, Bible stories, saints, religious holidays? What did you feel and think at the time of your baptism, first communion, confirmation? When and how do you pray? What do you call God? How would you like us to pray together?

Given that one is cooperating and not competing with the person's therapy, and that one has listened well before one spouts God-talk, there are then four things to consider about the ritual dimension of pastoral care for people with psychological problems or disorders. All four considerations apply to pastoral ritual care in general but take on a special urgency where a person is greatly confused or disturbed.

First, there is the basic human need to be seen as worth something, to be valued by another, a need which calls on one level for an assurance of God's love. As I have pointed out above, one powerful way to meet this need is by sacramental consolation, the appeal to the objective witness of the sacraments. Such an objective witness may be even more important to someone who cannot trust her internal voices. To a person who is convinced that she is bad and that God cannot love her, who discounts any positive thought or hope she might have as deceptive wishful thinking, there needs to come a voice from outside herself. "God adopted you in baptism, God wants to feed you at the Table." Such a person will not be able fully to internalize this message, to "believe" it within, without going through therapy or some other experience which transforms unconscious patterns. But she will still have a tangible, unchanging witness to another possibility, to a world which has a place for her as a valued individual, even if there is as yet no place in her to integrate that valuation. Every Sunday she is handed the certificate of adoption, even if there is as yet in her no frame or nail or wallspace where she can hang it up to stay.

A depressed or anxious person may obsess over his insufficient faith (after all, if he had sufficient faith, he wouldn't be depressed or anxious, right?), thinking that this lack bars him from the Kingdom. Here consolation may come through the role of the sacramental community. The pastor might say, "We are one bread, one body. No one can believe for himself all by himself. We believe together and for each other. There are times when each of us must rest on the faith of the community which carries us, as a baby does at its baptism." If the person's obsession is over his unworthiness to receive the sacrament and to participate in the sacramental community, there are again wonderful resources in Luther's writing. Luther was on the obsessive-compulsive side himself, and he "treated" his own obsessions of unworthiness, as some modern cognitive therapists would, with paradoxical thinking—but paradoxical thinking of great religious depth. The sense of unworthiness, for example, he declared to be a necessary prerequisite for worthy reception.

A second consideration is that images are easier to hold on to than abstract concepts. For someone whose emotional conflicts keep her from thinking clearly at times, the memorable character of symbols and religious images can be especially important. If you tell me, "Even if you don't live up to everyone's expectations or fulfill your potential, you are still valuable in God's sight," this sentence is not likely to stick with me in the dark night of the soul. If you tell me, "Even if you have fished all night and caught nothing, Jesus will come to you and cook you breakfast," there's a better chance. If we can then link jumping in the water with a return to sure identity and worth in baptism, and breakfast with the eucharistic meal, so much the better. The more symbolic richness an image has, the more roots it has in concrete aspects of experience, the easier it will be to hold on to in the midst of psychic confusion.

A third consideration of pastoral care for the emotionally troubled is the possibility that a specific "occasional" ritual may help meet deep emotional needs. The dramatizations in Gestalt therapy or in children's play therapy may have a ritual quality, as rites of blessing or farewell or expiation. A pastoral counselor, or a pastor working in cooperation with a parishioner's therapy, might help to bring about such rituals. For example: much emotional disturbance derives one way or another from unresolved grief; a ritual marking a loss one couldn't grieve in the past may allow one to move on. One woman, who entered therapy at 60, had never been able to grieve for her sisters, brother, and father, who had died in a murder/suicide tragedy when she was a child. For her, putting a marker at long last on the siblings' grave was an important ritual of grief which became the turning point in her therapy. The life and death of her brother and sisters no longer had to be denied; her grief was no longer unspeakable and could be integrated into her life, not only in the counseling room but by a public ritual statement. Other people may have had less catastrophic losses and yet need as she did to put a shape to their grief at last.

Other ritual possibilities might include a rite of baptismal renewal for someone who has suffered a loss of self (a loss of status or job, a disabling illness) and needs to experience his identity and vocation grounded in something deeper than the loss. Confession should be avoided if it seems to reinforce a self-assessment of badness. If practiced, the emphasis should be placed solidly on grace. A rite of healing might be appropriate in cases of serious conflict or distress, when healing is understood wholistically to apply to body, mind, and spirit. As with confession, however, the meaning of the "diagnosis" must be understood. In a nonfunctional family system where one member is focused on as "the problem," the "identified patient," a pastor would want to avoid praying for that person's healing if such ritual would play into the definition of this person as "the sick one." Requests for exorcisms, of course, should be met with a firm and caring referral to professional psychiatric care. One shouldn't have to say this, but unfortunately there are lots of people going around doing exorcisms these days. The real danger there is what happens when the ritual doesn't "work"; then the poor person (who is possibly borderline psychotic) has had his diagnosis of possession confirmed but the only hope for cure dashed. (In the worst abuses, the failure is blamed on the suffering person himself.) If defining psychologically based problems as sin or sickness can be problematic, defining them as demon possession is disastrous.

A far more common negative labeling of emotional disturbance defines it as a deficiency of faith. Many prayers written "for those in mental distress" imply this correlation, by asking God to "take away our doubts and fears, that we might trust you." One prayer in the new Lutheran *Occasional Services* book reads:

> O most loving Father, you want us to give thanks for all things, to fear nothing except losing you, and to lay all our cares on you, knowing that you care for us. Grant that fears and anxieties in this mortal life may not hide from us the light of your immortal love shown to us in your Son, Jesus Christ our Lord.[14]

This prayer maintains the Great Divide between God and self, with fear standing in between. It might be better to emphasize the incarnational more in all our praying, and especially in praying with those who feel deeply alienated from self and God. "In all their affliction God was afflicted, and the angel of God's presence saved them": the second half of that statement depends upon the first. That God hovers above the cloud of our anxiety is cold comfort. That God enters into our forsakenness is a far more transforming possibility, one which needs to be embodied more in ritual and in prayer.

In the next chapter the discussion will move to questions of alienation on a societal scale, as we consider issues of liturgy and social justice. On the large scale just as on the individual scale, however, some of the same concerns for pastoral ritual practice will be raised. Ritual must not be used to reinforce alienating labels or to avoid facing unsettling human needs. Rather, it must address human need honestly, in order to transform alienation into community.

CHAPTER 3

Ritual and Care
for
the World

RITUAL AS A FORCE
FOR JUSTICE

This book began with a discussion of the ideological split between the "ritualists" and the "counselors." This split led some pastoral counseling types to accuse ritual of being impersonal, rigid, and not responsive to individuals' feelings. Turning in this final chapter to the discussion of liturgy and justice, one would expect to escape this stereotyped objection to ritual, since the issues at hand are social rather than primarily individual in nature. In fact, however, one finds a similar split has been evident here up until recent times, a split between the "ritualists" and the "social activists." This split is as much a matter of stereotypes as the other, and as fundamentally unfounded. The "counselors" see ritual as forcing a rigid pattern onto personal experience; the "activists" may see it as reinforcing an unjust social order. Both groups see ritual as irrelevant or even detrimental to the fulfilling of the most important human needs. In the first two chapters I have shown how healthy ritual can meet the most personal of needs, for individuals and communities alike. In this chapter I shall explore the ways in which healthy ritual can be a force for social justice, in the institutional church and in the world the church serves. The fundamental argument remains the same: the more we know about important human needs, and the more we learn about how ritual can meet or frustrate those needs, the better we can design our liturgy to proclaim and embody the goodness of God's Reign—a reign of justice as well as love.

Ritual's Power for Order
and for Change

Some (*not* all) of the theologians who speak of solidarity with the oppressed are suspicious of the liturgy *per se*, and especially of the claim that liturgy can serve the world by embodying justice. Often they have had negative experience of the forms of the institutional church. Europeans may struggle with the problems of the established church and its legitimating of the state in rituals on civic occasions, while Latin Americans may react against the ceremonial accommodation between the official church and the oppressive ruling class. People anywhere may, as people have for centuries, see the rich accoutrements of sanctuary, vestment, and vessels as a mockery of the church's commitment to the poor, and a statement of where the church's heart really lies: invested in its own power of wealth and position. Such experiences help establish a dichotomy in people's minds between liturgy and social justice, between legitimating cult and liberating praxis, between conservative ritual and prophetic Word.

It is certainly true that ritual is in some sense an inherently conservative force. Its formalized pattern and its repetitions are meant to bring order out of the chaos of our lives, and to guarantee the continuity of this order over time: "as it was in the beginning, is now, and will be forever." In chapter 1 this creation of continuity was discussed as one of ritual's positive functions, with the caution that this goal is best served by a *flexible* order. Healthy ritual is never so rigidly defined as to be stagnant or completely unchanging. Even so, ritual does depend on order and sameness and resists sudden or radical change, and therefore it may be seen as a natural ally of the social status quo.

Some rituals, indeed, seem to be entirely directed at reinforcing the current social order. Civic ceremonies are frequently of this sort, self-congratulatory paeans to how good things are as they are, and how great we are in contrast to others. Yet even here the "conservative" force of ritual may be two-edged. If the ritual conserves the tradition, what does that tradition have to say? If the civic tradition embodies any ideals about freedom or justice in the society—if we sing at the baseball game about "the land of the free"—then the cause of liberation may not be wholly lost. The invocation of the ideal may be meant to imply that it is fulfilled in things as they are but there is nothing to prevent a participant from noting the discrepancy and feeling called to make good on the rhetoric.

The anthropologist Victor Turner has remarked on the great potential power of living rituals for change as well as for order. There is an experience of what Turner calls "communitas" in many rituals, an enactment of community or fellowship where usual status roles are suspended and all are temporarily equal. This experience is a radical challenge to the established order of society. That, according to Turner, is why ritual is hemmed about, clearly set apart from everyday life by the entry and exit rites and the boundaries of ritual space. It is as if you were encasing a radioactive isotope in lead, to prevent a chain reaction from running amok through the established order.[1] It is precisely because of ritual's radical potential that it must be so carefully ordered by society. Whether "communitas" is conceptualized within the official explanation of the ritual as a picture of the ideal order of equality or as a departure from the true order carried out with a special dispensation, its challenge to the society's everyday order is nullified when it is symbolically separated entirely from day-to-day existence.

There have been times and places where black and white Christians would never drink from the same cup—except at the Lord's Table. Such communion-sharing, if sufficiently separated from everyday life, could reinforce racism by tacit approval. "This is the only place," the ritual could be saying, "where you need to live out the equality of Christian brothers and sisters. It is a spiritual equality, appropriate to this spiritual place, and need not affect your interactions in the non-sacred world." The ritual enactment of equality in this way could actually quiet the conscience-stirrings of white Christians, by throwing their consciences a bone, a harmless gesture of right-mindedness. "Of course I know we're equal before God; I sit with them in church, don't I?" Yet the cup-sharing in church is only conceivable because it is absolutely, nonthreateningly separated from the eating at the family's dinner table, the drinking from the "white" fountain in the park.

The other possibility, of course, is that communion-sharing of blacks and whites together could act as a witness to how things should be in the everyday world. It could challenge people to conform our world to the Gospel order, that God's will might be done "on earth as in heaven." This is more likely to happen if the boundary between ritual and the secular world is allowed to be fairly permeable, so that everyday concerns have their place in the liturgy and the liturgical vision of community is continually applied to the secular world. This link is most explicitly made in preaching, of course; but there are ways in which other elements of the liturgy can resist "spiritualization" and segregation from the rest of life and can speak of justice without devolving into propaganda.

Two Maundy Thursdays

There are two fictional depictions of the same ritual, the Maundy Thursday foot-washing, which dramatically illustrate the two possible outcomes of the ritual expression of a counter-cultural ideal. In the 1978 Cuban film *The Last Supper*, directed by Thomas Gutierrez Alea, we see the dark side of ritual's relation to the power structures of society. The film shows a wealthy eighteenth-century planter deciding to emulate Christ's surprising action at the Last Supper by inviting some of his slaves to a feast at his manor and washing their feet. After the slaves have been thus "served" by their master, the drunken master promises these chosen ones that they need not work the next day, Good Friday. When they, believing him, refuse to work, they are beaten by the slave driver and realize that the master has forgotten his drunken promises. The slave driver is murdered, and the master wreaks a bloody punishment on the entire group.[2]

This is a particularly violent depiction of an idea which Victor Turner has expressed with regard to "rituals of reversal." Rituals of reversal are times when the usual status roles are voided and the social hierarchy is turned upside-down, as when in the medieval Feast of Fools the poor could taunt the lords with impunity. Turner, among others, holds that such rituals actually reinforce the social hierarchy by allowing a carefully contained catharsis of the revolutionary impulse. The film carries this thesis to its extreme, implying that the ritual symbols of Christian ideals actually lead to a worsening of oppression's brutal force, because the poor are manipulated by the symbols, made vulnerable through being misled into believing something the rich never really believed themselves.

The other side of the story, the opposite potential of ritual, is portrayed by Alan Paton in his novel *Ah, But Your Land Is Beautiful.*[3] A climactic scene in this novel is also a Maundy Thursday ritual. A highly placed white judge is invited to the black church of his family's housekeeper, where he participates in the foot-washing. As he is washing the housekeeper's feet, he thinks of the countless times she bathed his own children, washing and kissing them, and is moved to kiss her feet. The judge's presence and participation had been planned by the minister, and agreed to by himself, as a statement, but the kiss arises naturally within the ritual moment. Unlike the Cuban slave-owner, the judge is motivated by the deepest sense of mutuality and fellow-humanity, returning personal service for personal service. What is more, this reversal does not shore up the structure of oppression; rather, the society's assumptions are shaken to the roots. "It was the front-page story," writes Paton, "with great black headlines, like those that tell of war, or the eruption of Krakatoa, or a rugby victory over New Zealand. Even on Saturday morning it was still the big story, *Acting Chief Justice Kisses Black Woman's Feet*."⁴ The government is angry; it is now out of the question for the judge to be appointed chief justice. Yet while some whites feel threatened and insulted, others feel freed and proud, and the black minister sees a healing which could not have come through a thousand sermons.

Why does this ritual gesture bring grace and healing, where the slave-owner's brought only greater injustice? In part, one could say that the South African society is so vulnerable that it cannot allow even a symbolic enactment of an idea which threatens the system. So the society is itself responsible for the permeability of the boundary between ritual and secular space; it is a pressure cooker without the safety valve of securely contained rituals of reversal. Yet even if the South Africa of the 1950s could have allowed black and white to play out a safe, "spiritualized" equality in the church, it could not have stood for such an act as the judge's. For the more significant connection between ritual and everyday life is that made by the judge himself, when he looks at the housekeeper's feet and remembers her daily loving service to his children. In the Cuban story, the relationship of oppression has dehumanized the slaves in the eyes of their master, who cares nothing for the day-to-day reality of their lives, apart from their economic value to him. His ritual use of them is also dehumanizing, for he is deploying them as stage properties in the dramatization of his own delusionary self-image. The South African judge, in contrast, is not thinking of his own piety or liberalness at all, only of the other, who has served so long and whom he now has a chance to serve. It is a spontaneous, intimate, personal gesture which is nonetheless public, shared with the community, and deeply appropriate to the ritual's inner meaning. He is also not thinking of his own official position, but the fact that he was risking his career by this gesture of course gives it added credibility in others' eyes. He is not merely laying his privilege momentarily on the shelf, whence he can easily pick it up again; he is laying it on the line. All this keeps his act from being an "empty ritual gesture," and makes it a *full* ritual gesture, releasing the power of ritual to speak for justice and peace with force a thousand sermons could not equal.

These two fictional ritual events may seem too remote from our experience to be relevant to our questions of ritual practice. We do not live in the midst of such extreme forms of legalized oppression; we are not likely to have the opportunity to risk our professional future by a simple gesture of love in a Holy Week service. The issues that are highlighted in these dramatic examples, however, are the same issues which always arise when our rituals interact with structures of injustice. When we speak of justice for the oppressed, are we concerned with our self-image as charitable or liberal Christians, or are we really concerned with the oppressed? Is our ritual response to the needs of the poor comfortable or deeply challenging? Does it taste of condescension or of mutuality? Are the prayers and other ritual statements of concern cleanly separated off from the rest of life, from politics and social conditions, from daily interaction? Or are the connections clear in the community's life, as it struggles to conform its own order as well as the society's to the justice of God?

THE CRITICAL POWER OF
LITURGICAL MEMORY

The source of liturgy's power to challenge is in its memory. Liturgical remembrance is a unique sort of memory: a memory which does not just reminisce but re-presents, makes present; a memory which by recalling the promises of the past also recalls our future hope. The paradigmatic act of liturgical memory is the anamnesis of the eucharistic prayer, where the historical acts and future promises of God are recalled and re-presented in the act and promise of God's Christ in our midst, the covenant of bread and wine. Here we recall the history of Israel, of Jesus, and of the church as the history of God's self-giving. In this recollection we know who we are in the present: the outcome of God's creative love, the children of God adopted in baptism, the younger siblings of the Jews in the history of covenant, the followers of Jesus in the way of the cross. In this same recollection we also remember the promises God has made about our future, when Christ will come again and the reign of God will begin.

A memory of the past can transform the present and future. A prominent European theologian, Johann Baptist Metz, speaks of the "critical remembrance of suffering humanity." The word "critical" here means that the remembering challenges us to change the way things have always been, to question the structures of power that are established on human suffering. An uncritical remembrance of suffering is illustrated by the slaughter of Indians in the old cowboy movies. This memory of conquest simply reaffirms the divine right of the American order. A critical remembrance of the suffering of the Indians, in contrast, would call into question our national sense of mission and chosenness by demonstrating what extremes of injustice and bad faith and victimization can be cloaked by the rhetoric of this exalted self-image. This, in turn, can make us examine our national role in the present to see if we are similarly cloaking injustice in the rhetoric of national mission, and to find how we are perpetuating the injustices of the past.

One of the tasks of the church, in its liturgical life as well as in its formal education, is to recall the history of humanity in a different way than is usual in secular society. History is usually the story of the conquerors, where greatness is measured in wars won and peoples subdued. Will Cuppy had this in mind when he wrote of Alexander III of Macedonia: "He is known as Alexander the Great because he killed more people of more different kinds than any other man of his time."[5] The church, on the other hand, remembers a different sort of hero. The liturgical year commemorates saints who suffered unjustly, or who alleviated or prevented the suffering of others. July 4 is now the feast day of Isabel (Elizabeth) of Portugal, who prevented several wars by convincing her royal relatives to negotiate rather than set their peasants to slaughtering each other. Not a bad theme for our national holiday! Then there is Hugh of Lincoln, who refused to accept the office of prior until the king had housed and fully compensated every peasant who had been evicted in order to build the new monastery, and who alone faced down and quelled anti-Semitic lynch mobs, so that at times there were Jew-murdering riots in every major English city except his diocese of Lincoln. The suffering are recalled in the liturgy also, and not only those who suffered as a direct result of public admission of their Christianity. There are the innocent children slaughtered by Herod, representing all the anonymous "little ones" of history for whom Rachel weeps. There are the martyrs of the plague at Alexandria (262 A.D.), who stayed to care for the sick and fell victims to the plague themselves. Rather than see such people as human-interest sidebar stories in a history focused on the wielders of power, the liturgical calendar puts them in center stage of the history that matters.

Another way the liturgy presents an alternative to the secular view of history is by focusing on the authority and judgment of God above all human powers. When the liturgy ascribes all honor, power, and glory to God alone, it challenges all human claims to ultimate allegiance. This is the heart of the prophetic critique, which judges secular powers on the basis of divine norms, and that is why prophecy and worship are only at odds if worship has wavered from its true focus. The liturgy says in countless ways that God stands in judgment over all other authorities, and that our most essential loyalty is due to God alone. Sometimes, however, that witness is compromised by the uncritical use of national symbols in the liturgy. The national anthem is sung as if it were a hymn; the American flag is carried in procession along with the cross or displayed side by side with the "Christian flag." Then the ritual statement can appear to be that the nation deserves our equal allegiance, or at least that God supports the national interest. No matter how much we think the United States to be a force for good in the world, it is crucial to the maintenance of the church's independent and critical view of history that our patriotic feelings be clearly separated in ritual practice from our worship of the living God.

THE WITNESS OF
LITURGICAL ESCHATOLOGY

Perhaps the most striking difference in the church's view of history, though, comes in its view of the future. The church's eschatological expectation is neither a secular millenialism, where human progress or revolution will cure all, nor a spiritualized otherworldly-ism, where secular history is irrelevant because God will whisk us all Elsewhere. True Christian eschatology is a radical view of God's breaking into history here and now, in Christ, in Christ-in-us, to bring on the Reign of God, when the hungry will be fed, the mourners will be comforted, and the downtrodden will inherit the earth.

History-telling allows us to remember the injustices of the past; only liturgy allows us to remember the justice of the future. How can we remember what we have not yet experienced? In the Lutheran rite we sing that the eucharist is "a foretaste of the feast to come." That is the liturgical way of saying that the sacraments make the promises of God palpable, give them form, flavor, wetness, and the warmth of human touch. The sacraments are the embodiment of the "already" element in the "already–not yet" paradox of Christian eschatology. Will God turn our sea of chaos into living water to birth us and quench our thirst? We have seen it happen already, in the waters of the font. Will God feed us all, as Isaiah tells us, a feast of richest fare on the mountain of God? We have tasted it already, in the wine "drunk new in the Father's kingdom." Will God bring peace, lead us to the tree of life whose leaves will heal the nations, and abolish war forever? We have already known a community united by God's feeding, where the divisions of class and race and status and age are overcome, where the greeting of peace is extended from each to each, and where rich and poor, strong and feeble all receive an equal share in the abundant gifts of life.

This power of the sacraments to make the "already" palpable, to give a foretaste of the Reign of God, is a formidable witness to justice. At least since Paul wrote to the Galatians, the argument for justice and equality within the Christian community has been based on our common baptismal birthright. According to the world we may have been born to an unwed welfare mother or to the chairman of Exxon, but in baptism we have all been born of God, and each bears that highest dignity by grace alone. Prince Charles's son may be baptized from a silver heirloom bowl rather than the church's font, but even that symbol of distinction and class privilege cannot entirely obscure the common words and essence of the rite, which grant an inheritance no human parents could promise. When the only rights that matter are founded on sheer grace, earthly status can have no bearing on the structure of the community of God. It does, of course, intrude itself into the life of the church in countless invidious ways, but the point here is that baptism, by which we enter already into the community of God's future, is a constant witness against such divisions.

In a similar vein, Paul inveighs against the way in which the Corinthians perpetuate the divisions in the community even at the eucharistic meal. The Corinthians brought their own food for the feast, and the rich would eat and drink to excess while the poor went hungry. "You despise the church of God and humiliate those who have nothing," says Paul. "It is not the Lord's supper that you eat" (1 Cor. 11:20–22). To combat this practice, Paul, never at a loss for rhetoric of his own, turns instead to the tradition's story of the first Lord's Supper, the words of institution, as the most powerful argument at hand against the injustice at the Corinthian table. The words "This is my body" imply to Paul, among other things, the oneness of the community of those who partake of the one bread, and thus the abrogation of all distinctions within that community. To eat without discerning *that* body, that oneness, that sharing in Christ, is profanation. Even Paul couldn't always carry out the equality of the eschatological community in practice, enshrining as he did the male/female hierarchy in church life; yet the sacraments' witness to that equality remained to speak the "already" of the Reign of God.

The other side of the paradox of Christian eschatology is the "not yet." The "not yet" is equally important to the sacramental witness to justice, though in a different way. We worship in a world where many are starving, and we cannot feed them all at the congregation's table. The message of the eucharistic celebration, of the coming day when God will (in Ezekiel's words) "feed them in justice," is in itself a response to their plight. Yet we dare not celebrate the foretaste of that just meal in a glory untouched by the pain of the hunger that surrounds us.

This is what brings Gordon Lathrop to speak of the appropriateness of celebrating the eucharist as a "hungry feast," where we receive only a bit of bread and a sip of wine, where we sing the riches of God but go away still hungry, still thirsty. Lathrop appreciates the witness of the liturgy to the "already" of the Reign of God, the symbols' power to open up the possibility of an alternative world:

> And out of that imagination of an alternative may, in fact, come a humanized life, a life that moves toward freedom, a life that cries out earnestly for the day of God . . . and cries out in such a way that we begin to push against the rigid structures of our time and begin to require of them at least to approximate something more, something of God's gift in his coming kingdom.[b]

Such an alternative vision, says Lathrop, is the eucharistic meal, where the distribution of food is so different from the normal process in our world: not more for the rich and less for the poor, but an equal amount for all. This foretaste of an alternative reality, however, is shared in a hungry and unjust world. It was the awareness of the "not yet," as that is embodied in the pain of the world, which according to Lathrop led the early church to modify its eucharistic celebration. The food gathered at the assembly was redirected almost entirely to the poor, and only a little was saved out to enact the feast to come, when God would feed the world in justice. In this dual action the church maintained the tension of already and not yet. Our concern has to have this dual focus as well. While we work for justice in an unjust world, we must also enact the just community of God's future in our ritual. This ritual statement of hope is essential, even if all it can do is to awaken the hunger for a different way of being human; for when that hunger is awakened we stand in solidarity with all the truly hungry of our world.

LITURGICAL PREACHING
FOR JUSTICE

The most explicit confrontation with issues of social justice, along with all other ethical issues of our day-to-day living, takes place in the preaching. This statement should not be taken, however, to support any tendency to dichotomize the functions of preaching and liturgy, word and worship. The uneasiness of some contemporary theologians on the subject of formal liturgy can be traced in part to this unspoken set of dichotomies: prophetic vs. priestly, concrete vs. spiritualized, this-worldly vs. otherworldly, even "grass roots" vs. hierarchical. The main intent of this chapter is to move beyond this dichotomy by showing how the *whole* liturgy can act as witness and motivation to justice. As a part of that wholeness, let us first consider the power of preaching which makes use of liturgical symbol to speak for justice.

The core of all liturgical preaching for justice is the connection between liturgy and justice which is found in the biblical texts. If the preacher sees liturgical symbols as irrelevant to social issues, then she doesn't know enough about their biblical setting. Each of the central symbols of Christian liturgy bears within it a rich fund of biblical stories, many of which convey a strong message about the just order which God wishes to establish, and about our responsibility to our neighbors within that order. The liturgy can come to be cut off from social concern only if it is also cut off from its biblical roots, for the plant which grows from these roots will necessarily bear fruit in concern for the poor, the sojourner, the stranger, the outcast.

The Maundy Thursday foot-washing is a clear example of a liturgical action which speaks of God's order in its biblical setting. In fact, one might say that in John's account of the Last Supper, Jesus himself presents us with a paradigm of liturgical preaching for justice. "If I, your lord and teacher, have washed your feet, you also ought to wash one another's feet." Here Jesus draws out the meaning of his symbolic action by pointing out what it implies about relationships of power under the Reign of God. That I do this, he tells them, demonstrates that my lordship is an example of service. Similarly, the Lucan pericope in the Last Supper account where Jesus says, "I am among you as one who serves," connects the inversion of power relationships in the realm of God to Jesus' activity at the supper, where he serves the food to the disciples. Accordingly, the action of the "minister" in the liturgy, washing others' feet or serving them food, is biblically understood as a parable of the true evaluation of power and authority in the new dispensation. The leader becomes one who serves, the greatest becomes the least. Power must not be exercised as it normally is in the world we know; rather, authority must be understood as God's authorization to serve.

This same message about the inversion of our understanding of power is carried by many other liturgical symbols in their biblical context. To move a few days earlier in Holy Week, for instance, there is the processional of Palm Sunday, the reenactment of Jesus' entry into Jerusalem: the triumphal homecoming of a king to his capital, manifest in this humble, unlikely, unkingly arrival. Nor does the preacher have to wait until Palm Sunday rolls around to find a liturgical witness to this story of the inversion of expectations. At every eucharist we sing the greeting of the people of Jerusalem at Jesus' entry: Blessed is he who comes in the name of the Lord. In this Sanctus, in fact, we draw the contrast far more sharply than the people of Jerusalem could have, for we look not only for the royal authority their words attributed to Jesus, but for the power and majesty of the holy God whom Isaiah heard the angels praise. We sing the angels' "holy, holy" and the people's "hosanna," all to the one who came as a lowly, defenseless, death-bound man, and who comes to us now in the equally unlikely and humble fashion of one who serves at table.

This issue of the transformation of power relationships under God's Reign is only one of many important biblical themes of justice found in liturgical symbol. A few of the many layers of biblical associations dealing with power, justice, and the world's need can be easily demonstrated in relation to the central liturgical acts of the church, the sacraments of baptism and holy communion.

Eucharistic Symbolism
for Justice

The context for the Last Supper within the Gospel accounts is the place of meal-sharing in Jesus' total ministry. One of the most distinctive aspects of Jesus' ministry, the focus of followers' surprise as well as opponents' scorn, was his "eating with tax collectors and sinners." Jesus' table-sharing with those defined as unacceptable by social or religious community standards was, like his healing, an enacted parable about the truth of God's Reign. This breaking down of barriers was carried on into the early Christian communities, where slaves and landowners sat at table together, an unheard-of practice in Roman society. The point of this, though, went far beyond a sense of community within the Jesus-circle. The in-breaking of the Reign of God was meant to bring a radical change in living. As the healed person was told to "go and sin no more," so the person who sat at table with Jesus was impelled to change his or her life. The paradigmatic story here is that of Zaccheus. The persona non grata who hoped only to catch a glimpse of Jesus is astonished by his offer of table-fellowship, and receives him with joy. Perhaps Zaccheus is astonished, further, to hear himself promising to give half his goods to the poor. The cause-and-effect relationship is clearly implied. "Today salvation has come to this house," Jesus says, and the word "salvation" seems to stand for both events, the fellowship of Jesus himself, which announced to Zaccheus the Reign of God, and Zaccheus' response of joy and metanoia, shown in his commitment to the poor.

If we trace the imagery further through concentric rings, into the history of Israel, we find other meals that deepen our understanding of the context of care. Abraham's act of hospitality toward the three strangers is understood to have been received, in some mysterious way, by none other than the living God. The host finds himself more recipient than giver, receiving the promise of the one thing that meant life to him: the birth of a son. The tradition held Abraham's act of hospitality to be a powerful sign of care for those in need. The midwives in Egypt, according to a haggadic elaboration, decided on their act of civil disobedience—refusing to kill the male infants—by reminding themselves how Abraham went out of his way for total strangers. How could they not care for the helpless in their midst? The widow of Zarephath is also called on to act hospitably to a stranger, when Elijah is sent her way. While Abraham was rich in resources, she is preparing her last bit of food for herself and her child when she is asked to share it. Like Abraham, though, she finds that in feeding the stranger sent her by God, she is herself blessed with a gift of life: a promise of God's unfailing food, and the life of her son. "When did we see you hungry?" the perplexed subjects ask. The king tells them that when they have fed the least of these hungry ones, they have fed the king himself; and they receive far more than they gave, the inheritance of life.

Baptismal Imagery for Justice

Among the concentric rings of baptismal imagery in the tradition there is a similar story to tell. The Samaritan woman in John 4 is asked by a thirsty stranger for a drink, and finds herself receiving from this stranger the very water of life. Like the widow of Zarephath, this woman is an outsider to the community of Israel, but the living water washes away the ethnic and religious boundaries, even the social barriers of gender. A similar message is linked to baptism in the story of Peter and Cornelius. God has cleansed the world, Peter is told in the vision, and thus he understands that "God shows no partiality," and all have equal standing in the new dispensation. The water of baptism, Peter comes to appreciate, is a sign of the cleansing which God now extends in grace to all the world impartially, as an act of re-creating the world in justice.

The imagery of cleansing is as rich and varied as the imagery of feeding, but the connection with the call to care can be shown in just one of the many concentric rings of Old Testament images inherent in baptism. In Ezekiel 16, the city of Jerusalem is described as having been like an exposed infant, cast out on the open field to die in the blood of its birth. God found the infant Jerusalem, Ezekiel relates, and told her to live and grow up, washed her blood from her, anointed her, clothed and fed her. Ezekiel tells all this to convey God's judgment to Jerusalem: "You did not remember the days of your youth, when you were naked and bare, weltering in your blood," but turned to other gods and even "sacrificed your sons and daughters to them." You could not have sacrificed your children to your greed and lust for power, Ezekiel implies, if you had remembered how God cared for you, bathed you and clothed you, when you were like a helpless abandoned newborn. The bathing, clothing, and anointing of baptism can similarly be a symbol of God's care for us, helpless infants that we are in God's arms, and a call to remember that care in our care for the helpless.

The power of liturgical preaching is in images such as these. Words by themselves can easily become abstract, and the concept of God's care for us and for the world through us can be "spiritualized" into a sweet but unsubstantial goo. The liturgical enactment of God's care, by its own corporeality, but even more by the rich moral substance of its biblical imagery, can be a powerful reminder of our part in ringing in God's justice.

THE LITURGICAL SYMBOL
SPEAKS FOR ITSELF

It is common to think of the sermon as *the* place in the liturgy where the Gospel interacts with the issues of power and justice in our day-to-day world. While the most explicit application of the Gospel to the community's present situation is indeed made in the preaching, there are many other aspects of the total liturgy which have a bearing on issues of justice. Sometimes the cause-and-effect relationship between liturgical action and concrete social realities is far more direct than its homiletical counterpart could ever be. Some such relationships have already been suggested with reference to baptism, foot-washing, and the eucharist. In the rest of this chapter, I will take up six facets of liturgical action and community: the occasion and setting of the liturgy, the structure of the liturgical community, material things, inclusive language, the prayer for the world, and cultural adaptation of the liturgy. In each of these sections I will suggest some of the implications of this facet of liturgical practice for the pursuit of justice in the church and the world.

Occasion and Setting
the Liturgy

Due to the separation of church and state, the question of occasion and setting for the liturgy is a less acute one for American Christians than for Christians in other parts of the world. Europeans struggling with a state church background, for instance, must question the appropriateness of celebrating the eucharist publicly on civic occasions. The sort of nondenominational invocations that clergy are asked to give at our civic celebrations need not link the very heart of our faith with the good of the state or the club. In fact, the etiquette stipulates that we discretely sidestep the unique core of our own tradition and linger instead in the unthreatening pious penumbra of faith. My own favorite example of rhetoric overtaking meaning in such a context was a prayer delivered at the inaugural of a Chicago mayor, which asked that the mayor and community be led "by the pillar of cloud by day and the star by night." It sounded so good that no one seemed to notice the charmingly mixed metaphor: a truly "Judeo-Christian" prayer!

Yet even though state occasions in the United States are not marked by official celebrations of the eucharist, there remain other, uniquely American forms of civil religion in the church. A prime example of such an occasion is the civic feast of Thanksgiving Day. Established by presidential decree, this is the only day generally kept by American Christians as a religious holiday that does not have its origin in the church year. The celebration of Thanksgiving Day with a Christian liturgy is a ritual statement of the confluence of America's church life and its civil religion. There is more ambiguity, and probably more potential for creative tension, in this American emulsion of public piety and Christian faith than in the European or Latin American situations where church was dissolved into state. On the one hand, a Thanksgiving service can be a ceremony of national self-satisfaction, letting Christian rhetoric support our national "chosenness" in an uncritical way. It can express gratitude toward God for the blessings bestowed on our forebears in such a way that the blessings are seen as God's proper response to the early Americans' piety and hard work, and the message of our dependence upon God is lost. The celebration of abundance without a critical look at the need among us and throughout the world just reinforces the negative potential of the truly central ritual of the day, the family meal where all eat to excess. On the other hand, a Christian liturgy on this civil-religious occasion can complexify and critique the language of blessings and gratitude in a healthy way. The goal should not be an oppositional approach that tries to make everyone feel guilty for how much they will eat or how much America consumes. Rather, the liturgy should raise the questions of hunger, just distribution, and care for the earth as the natural moral dimension of the celebration of the good we have received and the recognition of our utter dependency upon God. F. Pratt Green's hymn "For the Fruit of All Creation" in the *Lutheran Book of Worship* is an excellent demonstration of this deepened sense of thanksgiving.

The most problematic issues of pastoral ritual care in nonecclesiastical settings arise for Americans in institutional chaplaincy. Chaplains always have to live with the tension between their identity as (lay or ordained) ministers of the church and their institutional affiliation. Even for hospital chaplains, who work within an institution with whose primary goal of healing the church is basically in agreement, there is tension. Should a chaplain wear the white uniform of the medical personnel, sharing in their image of professionalism, but also siding with an institutional system which the patient may find depersonalizing? For prison or military chaplains the tension can become much more acute. One of the realities of ritual function is that the chaplain, by his official presence and invocation, is perceived as legitimating or "blessing" whatever is going on around him. The prison chaplain is seen as placing the divine stamp of approval on the execution. The military chaplain is viewed as blessing the national cause or the slaughter of the enemy, as in the satire of Mark Twain. No matter how much chaplains may believe in the rightness of maintaining prisons or armies, they are faced with particularly delicate problems of ritually defining themselves as representatives of a more gracious, more just, more universal power than the one which pays their salaries. In what they wear, in the definition of the space in which they lead worship, in the language of their preaching and prayer they are constantly either identifying themselves with the institution or standing over against it. Nowhere is it harder for the Christian minister to integrate the prophetic and priestly roles.

Structure of the Community

When, as usually happens, the church determines for itself the occasion and setting for its liturgy, it does not thereby escape the issue of identification or tension with the power-structures of the culture at large. The most crucial way in which the power-relationships of the culture are replicated within the worshiping community is by the structuring of power and participation in the liturgical assembly itself. Who presides, who leads or participates in which activities, who participates only passively? Is the chancel filled with a phalanx of uniformed, white, middle-aged, professional men, like a corporate boardroom? Or is it occupied at various times by all sorts of people, of both genders and various ages, lay as well as clergy? Is the chancel—or the building, for that matter—accessible to the disabled? Do the cultural stereotypes hold in ritual roles, so that the respectable, dark-suited men tell people where to sit and when to move on, while their wives are expected to wash the communion vessels, and their children to be seen and not heard?

Church order, as that is manifest in the structure of the worshiping community, is itself a sign to the world of what the church is about. Objects and gestures and actions are not the only ritual symbols. The person handling the object or making the gesture is a symbol as well. At times the symbolic value of "who stands closest to God" becomes a dominant symbol in the ritual system, influencing the meaning of what is said or done. For instance, if the male language for God is always ritually intoned by men, the weight of gender-linked power, of authority-as-male, can become crushingly absolute. If the God-language remains male but is chanted and proclaimed also by vested women, behind the altar or in the bishop's chair, then the ritual statement is more complex and no longer univocally supports the essential maleness of holy authority. The little boy who saw his grandmother lead worship and reported excitedly, "Grandma was God today," gives us naïve evidence for this effect. One of my nieces, equally young but more sophisticated in religious language, gave another kind of witness to the impact of ritual roles. She had always "played church" as much as she'd played house; but when at the age of four she first saw a woman preside at the eucharist, she proceeded to start play that afternoon with the words: "Let's play *pastor*; I'll be Pastor Jan." Suddenly all the roles in the liturgy were available to her, including the authority of the presider.

There is no stronger witness to the inclusive message of the Gospel than a liturgical community where all the cultural assumptions associated with socioeconomic status, age, physical condition, gender, and race are playfully challenged in ritual practice. In such a community, you might see an eight-year-old who can read audibly acting as lector (when it's not even a "children's service"!), and receiving the respectful attention of hundreds of adults. You might notice whites in the gospel choir, or hear Spanish petitions in an English bidding prayer (or vice versa). As a hearing-impaired visitor, you might even find that the congregation has taken the trouble to learn how to sign the greeting of peace. In such a community, you may even find that men are just as likely to wash the dishes and women are just as likely to bless the assembly!

Material Things in the Liturgy

Aside from human bodies and their gestures, the material things most essential to Christian liturgy are the primary sacramental elements of water, bread, and wine. Sacramental theology has always had a great deal to say about the elements, their role in the communication of grace, and the rules for their composition and use. More and more in recent times, this discussion has been expanded to inquire how our use of material things in the liturgy bears on issues of ecology and social justice. From the beginning, the sacraments have linked Christians to the material, natural world, and helped offset "spiritualizing" tendencies which would deny the importance of the physical world. In this century there has been more systematic thinking about what a sacramental relationship to the matter of our existence implies for our ethics as well as for our patterns of prayer.

Water is pure grace. As a symbol of divine grace it is hard to beat. It comes down from above and wells up from beneath, giving life to the earth and all that grows on the earth. It is the medium of life's beginnings, in which we all floated before birth; we ourselves are mostly water. Water is a symbol of the givenness of nature, which precedes us and on which we depend. It is thus an appropriate symbol for the act of grace which initiates us into the body of Christ and the life of God.

There are various ways in which our ritual use of water can emphasize the symbolic message of our dependence on God's creative power. First, there can be enough water used so that it can appear as a medium, a surround, rather than a dab. The font can be large enough to suggest a womb, a bath, a tomb for Christians of all ages. If it is running water, "living" water, it speaks even more clearly of the fount of life, eternally springing up from a source we do not see.

The importance of this symbolism in a discussion of ritual care for the world is found in the recognition of our dependence on the medium of our life. Our customary attitude toward the natural world is an instrumental one, treating it as a collection of raw materials to be shaped to our ends. When we use water in this way without care or respect we pollute not only the rivers but the seas and even the rain. The water of baptism can serve as a ritual and homiletic sign of God's creative gift, in nature as well as in grace, on which we are so utterly dependent. That knowledge of dependence should lead us to care for the natural world which bears us, washes over us, surrounds us on every side.

The bread and wine of the eucharist stand as a more complex symbol, because they are not simply given in nature. They are natural substances transformed by human labor; the Roman Catholic liturgy speaks of the bread "which earth has given and human hands have made." The way we use these products in liturgy thus speaks of our relationship not only to the natural world but also to the social and economic world of food production. As a church which baptizes cannot logically be indifferent to the pollution of the earth's water, so a church which celebrates the eucharist cannot ignore the plight of the wheat farmers or the migrant grape pickers.

There is a story about bread and justice told of the sixteenth-century saint Francisco Solano, who preached in Peru and Argentina. When some conquistadores invited him to eat with them, he took the bread in his hands, squeezing it until blood began to ooze from it. He told them, "This is the blood of the Indians," and returned to his convent without eating a mouthful, later explaining he could not eat bread kneaded with the blood of the oppressed.⁷ The bread and wine of our celebrations do not have such a dramatic tale of oppression to tell as the enslavement of the Indians. Nonetheless, like Francisco Solano, we must care about the source of the bread we bless, not only praying thanks for their labor but caring about the conditions of their labor. A man in my church asked one Sunday why the wine tasted different and was told matter-of-factly that we had stopped using Gallo port because of the boycott. He said later that it had never occurred to him before to consider where the wine came from, and who picked the grapes; the symbol had raised for him an issue of justice.

The type of bread we use is also a statement about nature and human labor. Happily, the liturgical movement's sensitivity to symbolic power has influenced some communities to begin using bread which is recognizable as bread. The stamped-out, tasteless wafers with which most of us are familiar seem more a product of machines than something "which human hands have made." They are more de-natured than supermarket bread, more standardized than fastfood burgers. They throw the weight of holiness behind the omnipresent alienation between us and the nature that feeds us, between us and the works of our hands. Any move in the direction of a bread which tastes of wheat and looks like a human product is a step toward bridging this alienation, which underlies so much of our ecological and economic patterns of abuse.

If members of the congregation make the bread, that is an even firmer bridge, a closer experience of our dependence on others' labor for our taste of God. The baker might be ritually honored for his labor. For example, he might bring the bread up to the altar in the offertory procession, and instead of letting the ushers take it along with the money, the celebrant herself might come down to receive it, with a deep bow to the baker. The best symbol of all might be for the whole community to take turns baking the bread. Despite the mystique to the contrary, breadbaking is something nearly anyone can do, particularly if paired at first with a knowledgeable partner. One woman said that the first time bread she had baked was used for the Sunday eucharist, she had quite an unexpected and powerful reaction to the sight of her bread lifted at the consecration. She characterized that reaction as wonder that the ordinary work of her hands could be transformed into the means of God's presence for the community. "Suddenly," she said, "all those things I'd heard about the doctrine of vocation came home to me." There is no better argument for the dignity of human labor than this.

In addition to people, water, bread, and wine—the only material things necessary for Christian assembly—there are countless other physical accoutrements of worship. The richness of vestment and vessel and architectural adornment has long been one of the facts adduced to argue the hypocrisy of all the church says about caring for the poor. With the righteousness of the disciples scolding the woman who anointed Jesus, many people have argued that money spent on the "things" of worship is misplaced, and has more to do with institutional pride than with the glory of God. Anyone who has spent time in a congregation that lived for its building program alone will appreciate the strength of this argument. The other side of the story, however, is that symbols work in ways that elude precise economic assessment. They can bond communities together across class lines; they can inspire service and social action; they can evoke the perfect justice and harmony of the Reign of God.

Some communities have found successful ways of welding together their concern for the poor and their adornment of the house of God. The most famous recent story of this kind is that of the Episcopal cathedral of St. John the Divine in New York City. In the 1960s the bishop stopped the building program in progress and declared that the cathedral would not be finished as long as there were still poor and hungry people living in its shadow. That in its way was a strong symbol of concern for justice. The next bishop took a different tack, however, and decided to start a program training unemployed city-dwellers as stonemasons to finish the cathedral towers. Another community which similarly found a way to combine its investment in worship and its concern for justice is a Lutheran church in Connecticut, which went through the usual debates as it considered buying a tracker-action organ. Is it right to spend so much money on this when people are homeless and hungry? Their decision was to refrain from buying the organ until they had raised twice its cost, with the extra money designated to support low-income housing for the elderly in the church's neighborhood. Thus the organ became the symbol in people's minds of this community's care for the world.

Inclusive Language

The issue of inclusive language is currently the most visible and dis-. cussed of all the issues of justice in worship. There are so many fine studies of the question available that I will not address the question at length. Instead, I will merely formulate two principles to be considered in any discussion of language in litany and lectionary.

The first principle is that language has immense, pervasive, and subtle power. Because it is the vehicle of all human construction of meaning, it has great power to shape our conscious and unconscious images of ourselves and the world around us. This power must be acknowledged, respected, and monitored. We must find ways, as part of the pastoral task, to understand the effect of our religious language on ourselves and to listen respectfully to others' experience of its effect on them. Adult education classes can be a good forum for this; rather than focus on the "controversy" of inclusive language, it might be better for the participants to explore the nature and development of their own religious imagery together. The prime directive in any such discussion is to remember that the effects of language, like those of any taken-for-granted structural force (gravity, the beams of a house), remain unconscious until they are called into question by a countervailing force (a leap upward, an earthquake). This means that those people for whom the male pronoun or darkness imagery is not problematic should not dismiss the concerns of those who are disturbed. If language were as neutral as binary digits, then metaphors for God would indeed be arbitrary, and individuals' emotional associations irrelevant. As language is not neutral, but carries a whole social history in each word, one must listen to how it affects the *whole* church— particularly those groups who have not had the power to shape our social history.

The second principle is that our language, since it is not neutral but colored by history, can never be "pure" and free from all oppressive potential. Any metaphor for God from human experience will evoke ambivalent associations for all and memories of suffering for some. This is as true of "sister" or "friend" as it is of "father" or "king." The reason why "father" and "king" have more oppressive potential is that they name roles of greater power—men on whom others have been extremely dependent, needing what only they had to give. When human beings have others dependent upon them, they tend to aggrandize themselves by subjugating their dependents. That God does not do this—despite the greatness of our need for what only God can give—is the meaning of grace. The inadequacy, even self-contradictoriness, of all our metaphors for grace is the inevitable condition of speech in a fallen world.

The point here is not to deny that some words are far more oppressive than others, given our social context. Some things are indeed too full of oppressive potential to be said in Christian worship: "the Jews plotted to kill him" is one example. The point is, rather, that "offense" cannot be the sole criterion for the choice of liturgical language. If we removed every image that could offend, we would be left with a printout of 0s and 1s. The Puritans tried to abolish images, and ended up despite themselves creating a most powerful artistic symbol: the pure white, simple, straight-lined church. We would generally be better off using a system of checks and balances, creating new symbols (or expanding on existing ones) that counterpoint the dominant-culture symbolic of the Great White Father-King and His Favorite Sons, the Priests. Instead of having the confirmation class pick a single "class hymn," for instance, one might have them make a collage of hundreds of images of God: mother, father, infant, friend; bread, tree, supernova, ocean; monarch, servant, protestor, hostess, clown. We have a far better chance of achieving a richer symbolic than of producing a "pure" one.

The Prayer of the Church

The prayer of the church in the eucharist, or the "pastoral prayer" in some Protestant services, is the main place outside the sermon where the concerns of the world become the ritual focus. To be ritually honest, this prayer must do what it claims to do: lay before God the problems of the world and plead for divine presence, help, blessing, and life. Many such prayers have a (barely) hidden agenda, which is to tell the congregation what they are to feel and do about the problems of the world. Under the guise of addressing God they prescribe feelings of guilt, concern, or joy, and sometimes the proper course of social action as well. As to prescribing feelings, the danger of subjectivization was pointed out in the first chapter's discussion of ritual honesty. As to prescribing a specific course of action, that is better saved for the sermon, where it can be done straightforwardly, not underhandedly. The pastoral task here is to lead the assembly in prayer, not to instill moods or to moralize.

If we assume that the pastor is really leading the community in prayer, the issues of morality and justice do not disappear; they merely become more profound. Real prayer will eventually affect our attitudes, even if our mood never meets the presider's expectations. Real prayer will change the way we see the world and our place in it, and thus will impel us to act for justice, though perhaps in a way quite different from the minister's pet project.

The prayer of the church can create quite a different vision of the world from that which we see on the television news. The list of tragedies brought to us nightly on the news can easily overwhelm us. True, a discrete crisis such as a natural disaster may motivate us to send money: the relief will help, and the hurricane is not likely to return next week to make it all futile. In contrast, the recurring tragedies with wider political and social causes—torture, war, terrorism, oppression—are likely to make us feel hopeless and powerless, to make us want to distance ourselves psychologically from the people to whom such things happen. Prayer recasts the world with all its tragedy by placing it in relation to the cross. Once I asked a friend what the cross meant to him, and after a pause he answered: "It allows me to take the whole world seriously." That is what a good prayer of the church does; it takes the whole world seriously, by way of the cross. We look into the heart of darkness and see the heart of God. We hear the cry of the godforsaken and respond, "Truly these are the children of God."

It is the juxtaposition of the human situation with the cross which brings both prophetic judgment on all who inflict unjust suffering and the eschatological hope of God's hidden presence. The pastor can try to spell out what exactly this calls us to do in her sermon, but in the prayer she should let the cross speak. Her pastoral task here is to make sure that the community prays for the whole world, not just those for whom it feels comfortable to pray. This may mean praying for strikers when the majority of the congregation sides with the management, or for scabs in a congregation of union members. It always means remembering the forgotten of the world, the "little ones" whose suffering is not newsworthy because it is such an everyday, ongoing occurrence. In the prayer of many Lutheran churches in this country in recent years, the political oppression of fellow Lutherans in Namibia has been brought to the community's attention week after week, whether or not it was in the news. This sustained concern has brought consequences in social action that are rooted deep in a sense of community with the suffering. We pleaded their need along with ours so long that the two needs came to seem linked. The prayer of the church is for the sake of the world, but it will have done its work on us as well when it makes us beggars, with the suffering ones, for the justice of God.

Cultural Adaptation of
the Liturgy

The final issue of liturgical witness to justice is as much a concern of the worldwide church and the ecumenical movement as it is of the local community, but however large-scale, it remains a quintessentially pastoral task. This task is the balancing of a passion for unity in the church with a respect for the diversity of cultures and denominational and ethnic traditions. Both of these serve justice in different ways. Sharing ritual does strengthen worldwide community. That these words are spoken, this cup lifted, unites us palpably with Christians the world over as sisters and brothers, born of the same waters, fed on the same food. Respect for diversity, on the other hand, serves justice by giving the different cultural voices in the church an equal hearing, and seeing the Spirit at work in the new as well as the old.

Since this is a clash of goods, it can lead to particularly painful choices. Take a central symbol for an acute instance: bread and wine. For some people bread and wine are totally alien foods, and many have argued that such people ought to be able to hold eucharist with their own staple foods, which they experience as the staff of life: rice, or coconut, or whatever. There is undeniably good in people's sacramental experience of Christ's coming to them as *their* food. Yet the loss is also great: the good of the symbolic worldwide unity found when "we who are many are one body, for we eat of the one bread." They gain the symbolic multivalency which their staple food possesses in their culture and language, and lose the centuries of metaphoric play with the symbols of bread and wine in the Christian tradition. Conflicts such as this are inevitable in a culturally pluralistic church with a history-conscious faith.

There is no way to pare Christianity down to an essential ahistorical core free of cultural bias, just as there is no way to purify a historical text of all metaphors tainted by the history of human oppression. Any attempt to do this definitively would leave one with a bare concept of "love" or "equality," stripped of all historical concreteness, as well as all symbolic richness. Here, as in the matter of language, the better way to counter bias is to add layers of meaning to the historically conditioned, common symbolic core of word and font and table. Then, though we may not all use the same music or patterns of assembly, we can all be enriched and challenged by each other's divergent styles of prayerful gathering around that common center. Roman Catholics singing "A Mighty Fortress" may pick up the best of Lutheran piety: its biblical richness, its emphasis on faith as trust. Lutherans singing spirituals may learn to take more seriously the relation between the freedom of the Gospel and the longing of the oppressed. Westerners watching an Asian pastor bow to his congregation at the greeting "The Lord be with you" may learn something of the deep mutual respect which the words of that exchange imply. This process of mutual critique and enrichment is the best gift of pluralism to the worship of the universal church.

LIBERATING RITUAL

This chapter has suggested a great variety of ways in which the church's liturgy can be a voice for God's justice. It should be clear by now that liberating ritual is not propagandistic ("O God, make us see that our policies in Central America are wrong"). Rather, ritual acts as a liberating force when it reflects in all its parts the loving justice of the Reign of God. The simple fact of a woman's celebrating, for example, can be revolutionary in people's lives, challenging their assumptions about sexual hierarchy or freeing women from oppressive self-concepts. In *God's Fierce Whimsy,* Mary Pellauer describes her first experience of seeing a woman preside at the eucharist.[8] She tells how the sight of a woman lifting the cup of red wine, of holy blood, healed something deep in her, by counteracting all the messages about the impurity and ugliness of woman's blood. Here was a woman consecrating the blood of the new covenant for the life of the community: the liberation extended its blessing even to the culture's unconscious association of menstruation with uncleanness and danger. Nothing rivals the power of ritual to liberate on so many levels at once, from the unconscious ambivalence about blood to the public sphere of gender stereotypes and social hierarchy.

Even the most private of rituals and the simplest of gestures can be forces for justice, when they reflect God's Reign. One woman provided me with such a story about confession. This woman had had much experience in her life with male clergy who were invested in hierarchical power, and who thought that the proper place of women in the church was kneeling at men's feet, being fed, blessed, absolved, or churched after childbirth. Still valuing the discipline and grace of the sacrament of reconciliation, however, she went to a priest she knew and trusted as one who would speak from the authority of the Gospel promise rather than from the power of his own position. They sat on low chairs for most of the rite, and then the priest moved to extend the absolution. Being a tall man, he quite naturally, without premeditation, knelt by her in order comfortably to put his hands on her head. Quite unexpectedly this woman, like Mary Pellauer, felt something healed in her: the resentment and self-debasement of years of being required to kneel before consecrated men. For the first time in her experience, absolution was clearly not an exercise of hierarchical power over her, but a movement in grace to meet her. It was a movement which came through a kind of hierarchy, surely, for the man's ordination gave his words the ritual weight of the church's surety. But the ritual hierarchy was subject to a prior truth, the mutuality of service in love. The hope for the church's life is that we might all, like this priest, live that truth so well that we enact it unconsciously in our liturgies, transforming them into rituals of liberation for individuals and for the world.

Notes

INTRODUCTION

1. H. P. V. Renner, "The Use of Ritual in Pastoral Care," *Journal of Pastoral Care* 23 (September 1979): 165–66.

2. Victor White, quoted in Robert Hovda, *Dry Bones* (Washington, D.C.: The Liturgical Conference, 1973), 59.

3. Paul Pruyser, "The Master Hand: Psychological Notes on Pastoral Blessing," in William B. Oglesby, Jr., ed., *The New Shape of Pastoral Theology* (Nashville: Abingdon Press, 1969), 352-65.

4. Gordon Lathrop, "On Bringing the Ark from Ashdod to Jerusalem," *Response* (Pentecost 1973): 7.

CHAPTER 1

1. This letter appeared with the name of the writer withheld by request in *The Lutheran* (September 7, 1983): 33.

2. Erik Erikson, *Toys and Reasons* (New York: W. W. Norton, 1977), 88.

3. See Gordon Lathrop, "A Rebirth of Images: On the Use of the Bible in Liturgy," *Worship* 58 (July 1984): 291–305.

4. Erikson, *Toys and Reasons,* 89.

5. Arnold van Gennep, *The Rites of Passage* (Chicago: The University of Chicago Press, 1960).

6. Victor Turner, *The Ritual Process* (Ithaca, N.Y.: Cornell University Press, 1977).

7. Thomas G. Simons, *Blessings for God's People* (Notre Dame, Ind.: Ave Maria Press, 1983).

8. Van Gennep, *The Rites of Passage,* 11–12.

9. E. Glenn Hinson, "Baptism, A Southern Baptist Dilemma," *Liturgy* 4 *(Putting on Christ,* Winter 1983): 41.

10. Thomas Droege, "The Formation of Faith in Christian Initiation," *The Cresset* (April 1983): 16–23.

11. Hinson, "Baptism, A Southern Baptist Dilemma," 41.

12. John H. Westerhoff III and William H. Willamon suggest Christian vocation as a focal theme for a rite of adult confirmation in their book, *Liturgy and Learning Through the Life Cycle* (New York: The Seabury Press, 1980), 80–86.

13. John O. Nelson (personal communication).

14. *Ritual in a New Day* (Nashville: Abingdon Press, 1976) was produced by the Task Force on the Cultural Context of Ritual as part of the Alternate Rituals Project of the Section on Worship of the Board of Discipleship of the United Methodist Church. The reference here is to the "Ritual in Which Both Spouses Participate," 91.

15. Westerhoff and Williamon, *Liturgy and Learning Through the Life Cycle*, 131.

16. Ibid., 124.

17. Thomas Droege (personal communication).

18. For a divorce ceremony which focuses on the expression and resolution of personal feelings, see Sam Norman, "A Ceremony for the Divorced," *Journal of Pastoral Care* 33 (March 1979): 60–63.

CHAPTER 2

1. Paul Pruyser, "The Master Hand."

2. Amy Schwartz, *Mrs. Moskowitz and the Sabbath Candlesticks* (Philadelphia: The Jewish Publication Society of America, 1983).

3. For a fuller account of issues of assessment and pastoral response in the sacrament of reconciliation, see Clark Hyde, *To Declare God's Forgiveness* (Wilton, Conn.: Morehouse Barlow, 1984).

4. See especially Charles Gusmer, *And You Visited Me: Sacramental Ministry to the Sick and the Dying* (New York: Pueblo, 1984), as well as *Liturgy: Ministries to the Sick* (vol. 2, no. 2).

5. Jerome Berryman, "The Rite of Anointing and the Pastoral Care of Sick Children," in Diane Apostolos-Cappadona, ed., *The Sacred Play of Children* (New York: The Seabury Press, 1983), 63–77.

6. Gwen Kennedy Neville and John H. Westerhoff, III, *Learning Through Liturgy* (New York: The Seabury Press, 1978), 172.

7. Eda LeShan's book, *Learning to Say Good-By* (New York: Avon, 1976), gives several examples of children's own chosen ways to ritualize their grief.

8. Susan Borg and Judith Lasker, *When Pregnancy Fails* (Boston: Beacon Press, 1981), 141.

9. Ronna Case, "When Birth Is Also a Funeral," *Journal of Pastoral Care* 32 (March 1978): 6–21.

10. Harry Pritchett, Jr., "One Egg Was Empty," *The Lutheran* (April 6, 1983): 10–11.

11. Muriel M. Carder, "Spiritual and Religious Needs of Mentally Retarded Persons," *Journal of Pastoral Care* 38 (June 1984): 143–54.

12. Oliver Sacks, *The Man Who Mistook His Wife for a Hat* (New York: Summit Books, 1985).

13. Ibid., 36.

14. *Occasional Services,* a companion to *Lutheran Book of Worship* (Minneapolis: Augsburg Publishing, House, 1982), 60.

CHAPTER 3

1. Victor Turner used this metaphor in a lecture given at the University of Chicago in the fall of 1982.

2. I owe this description to Volney Gay's "Ritual and Self-Esteem in Victor Turner and Heinz Kohut," *Zygon* 18 (September 1983): 271–82.

3. Alan Paton, *Ah, But Your Land Is Beautiful* (New York: Charles Scribner's Sons, 1982).

4. Ibid., 235.

5. Will Cuppy, *The Decline and Fall of Practically Everybody* (Boston: Nonpareil Books, 1950, 1984), 38.

6. Gordon Lathrop, "The Eucharist as a 'Hungry Feast' and the Appropriateness of Our Want," *Living Worship* 13 (November 1977).

7. Enrique Dussel, "The Bread of the Eucharistic Celebration as a Sign of Justice in the Community," in Mary Collins and David Power, eds., *Can We Always Celebrate the Eucharist?* (*Concilium* 152; New York: The Seabury Press, 1982), 60.

8. Mud Flower Collective, *God's Fierce Whimsy* (New York: The Pilgrim Press, 1985), 132.